ASPERGER'S SYNDROME

ASPERGER'S SYNDROME

When Life Hands You Lemons, Make Lemonade

Anita A. Lesko

iUniverse, Inc.
Bloomington

Asperger's Syndrome
When Life Hands You Lemons, Make Lemonade

iUniverse books may be ordered through booksellers or by contacting:

iUniverse
1663 Liberty Drive
Bloomington, IN 47403
www.iuniverse.com
1-800-Authors (1-800-288-4677)

ISBN: 978-1-4620-3052-1 (sc)
ISBN: 978-1-4620-3053-8 (e)

Library of Congress Control Number: 2011911596

Printed in the United States of America

iUniverse rev. date: 08/01/2011

Dedication

I dedicate this book to my mother, Rita, who enabled me to become the person I am today, and for everything I've accomplished throughout my life. She has always believed in me and encouraged me to work hard and follow my dreams, no matter how far-fetched they seemed to be. I've always dreamed big, and she's right there to cheer me on. Because we didn't know I had Asperger's syndrome when I was a child, indeed there were endless struggles with my "Asperger ways," but somehow, she instinctively knew exactly what to do with me to keep me calm and focused. I can well remember endless times of getting upset or stressed out over something, but she always remains calm and works to bring me back to my natural state of peace and calmness. She has devoted her whole life to me, and because of that I have accomplished things that others only dream of, because I focused on the gifts that I was given when I was born with Asperger's.

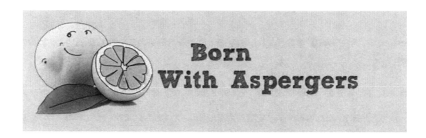

Visit Anita Lesko's website at
<u>www.bornwithaspergers.com</u>

Contents

Foreword

Asperger's syndrome is poorly understood by most people. In fact, many people in the medical and mental health fields truly do not comprehend the magnitude of the challenges that people with Asperger's face, much less how to help them. Society is now becoming more aware of this problem, but we have a long way to go. It has been estimated that as many as 50 to 100 million people worldwide might have Asperger's. This syndrome is on the autism spectrum, a very high-functioning version. People with Asperger's usually have above average intelligence, and often are in the genius category. Famous people who may have had Asperger's syndrome include Albert Einstein, Wolfgang Amadeus Mozart, Thomas Jefferson, Thomas Edison, and Charles Lindbergh; and in our time, possibly Bill Gates and Dan Aykroyd. Society's interest has primarily been in trying to treat people with Asperger's as if they have a mental disability, rather than educating the rest of us about how we can be more accommodating. Unfortunately, only limited resources are available to help these individuals, and even finding a support group can be difficult. However, this book gives us a greater understanding of the challenges our fellow human beings with Asperger's are forced to confront. Anita Lesko's story and her struggle for acceptance make us realize that we are all part of the same human family.

I have known Anita Lesko for a few years, and after hearing her story, I was excited to see it in print. She tells her story about living with Asperger's syndrome in a positive, life-changing way. She begins with many of the most memorable events that occurred early in her life, which molded her into the person she is today. She continues by showing us how complex the challenges can be for an adult with Asperger's in the workplace and in relationships. Through her examples of how she faced adversity throughout her life, Anita shows us that we are all capable of making a difference, no matter what our unique circumstances are. Anyone struggling with a social-skills problem like Asperger's syndrome will be able to relate to and learn from her experiences. Anita's story will also help those of us who do not have Asperger's understand the emotional and interpersonal difficulties they experience, in a way that will help us better understand them and hopefully accommodate their unique needs. This is not simply another book about another obscure medical disorder. This is a book about change and overcoming adversity. It's about helping others achieve a better life.

Anita's accomplishments are many, including earning a master of science in nurse anesthesia from Columbia University, becoming an internationally published military aviation photojournalist, and numerous other achievements, including a support group she started for people with Asperger's syndrome. She encountered constant obstacles all along the way, which is why Anita's story is so inspiring, and is a great example of the resilience and determination of the human spirit.

I have worked in the mental health industry for over twenty years and have had the opportunity to work with many people who have Asperger's syndrome. Too often I've seen the person with Asperger's treated as if he or she is permanently disabled and incapable of participating in normal life. People with Asperger's often have difficulty maintaining relationships with others and have problems in the workplace due to the social challenges they face. They also experience frustration on a different scale than most of us realize. As a result, they are often pushed to the fringes of our society and never feel fully accepted as equals.

Anita has presented her story so the reader can experience the emotions of many of her life challenges, while instilling a message of hope and healing for us all. This book is truly an inspiration for those with Asperger's syndrome, their families, educators, and simply anyone who enjoys reading about overcoming adversity to achieve some very lofty goals. Anita has truly made lemonade out of lemons!

Brett W. Turner, PsyD
Clinical Neuropsychologist

Introduction

Recently I watched Oprah Winfrey on a show talking about her best friend Gayle King. Oprah was discussing how wonderful it was having Gayle in her life and how great it is to have a best friend. I started to cry because I have never had a friend. I have Asperger's syndrome, and not having friends is a normal aspect of your life with this syndrome. As I continued to listen to Oprah, I realized that it was necessary to write this book. In addition to everyone with Asperger's syndrome, this is for their families, associates, educators, and employers. It is also for anyone who is different. I want to educate America, educate the world, about Asperger's syndrome and what it is like to have it.

Although this is a memoir about my life with Asperger's syndrome, it is also meant to be a motivational and inspirational journey as the reader walks in the shoes of someone with Asperger's. I have included a chapter in which I offer advice to everyone with this syndrome, the parents of children with Asperger's syndrome, and educators. I was nearly fifty years old when I found out I had Asperger's, and this gives me a unique perspective. I can look back and analyze every step I took, allowing me the ability to offer advice and guidance to others in my situation. My goal is to help others with Asperger's syndrome, to provide the hope and encouragement that you are just as capable of leading a rich, exciting, and productive life as everyone else. It is also meant to be an inspiration to anyone who is different, in whatever way that might be. For anyone who has ever been bullied, you will find a connection here, because I have been bullied my entire life, not only as a child and teen, but in the workplace as well.

You will be taken into the mind of someone with Asperger's syndrome. If you don't have Asperger's, you will see that it is not a disease, but instead a way of life. The brain of an Aspie, as someone with Asperger's is called, is wired differently from normal (neurotypical) people. Yes, we are different, but we are not less.

The account of my life that follows shows that I focused on the gifts that I was given, rather than on my limitations.

I will take you along on my journey through life with a syndrome I didn't know I had until two years ago, as I was nearing my fiftieth birthday. That was a long time to live without knowing I had Asperger's syndrome. It affected every interaction with every person I met over all those years. It affected every decision I made, every path I chose to go down, only I didn't know the driving force behind it all. When I got interested in something, I would have a laser focus on working tirelessly until I accomplished my goal. Even I could not explain the drive I had for these special interests.

This invisible force also rendered me incapable of interacting with people successfully. I always felt like I was on the outside looking in. No matter what my heart wanted, my head didn't allow it to happen. Now I know what that force is: Asperger's syndrome. I found I have it only by chance. A coworker had been having problems with her son, Gary, for several years. She took him to a neuropsychologist when he was six, and the child was diagnosed with Asperger's syndrome. The next day she told me about Gary's diagnosis and handed me some literature about Asperger's. I started reading the information, and suddenly everything around me seemed to fade. It was as if the person who wrote the literature had known me from the instant I was born. Tears welled up in my eyes, and I got a lump in my throat. That night I stopped at the bookstore on my way home from work to get every book they had about this syndrome. The first book I read was by Dr. Tony Attwood, *The Complete Guide to Asperger's Syndrome*; and as I read the book, I felt like he knew me since I was four years old. I stayed up all night reading it, mostly crying but often laughing. It was the ultimate *aha* moment, when all of the pieces of the puzzle fell into place. The aspects of my life that I never understood, like why I was so different, why I never fit in anywhere, why I could never make any friends, were finally solved. I have Asperger's syndrome. It was unbelievable.

I made an appointment with the same neuropsychologist my coworker's son had gone to, Dr. Brett Turner, to get a formal diagnosis.

In 1988 I graduated from Columbia University in New York City with my master of science in nurse anesthesia. I earned my bachelor of science in nursing from Bloomfield College, which was in my hometown of Bloomfield, New Jersey. After graduating from Columbia University, I started working as a CRNA, a certified registered nurse anesthetist, and have been working full-time ever since, now going on twenty-four years. I've specialized in anesthesia for transplants, including liver, heart and lungs, kidney, and pancreas. Eventually, my interest shifted to neurosurgery, and I've done a lot of anesthesia for brain tumors, aneurysm clippings, and spinal fusions.

As a child I got hooked on horses at an early age, somewhere around two years old, with my first pony ride. That passion has lasted a lifetime, eventually leading to jumping horses over six-foot high fences in big competitions. My parents didn't have money to buy me a horse or riding lessons, so I became a working student at a riding stable near my home when I was about twelve. This was my first special interest. I had high aspirations to become a top-level rider, and I literally worked my way up the ranks, shoveling out stalls, picking rocks out of paddocks, painting fences, whatever needed to be done to earn yet another ride, another lesson.

If I hadn't developed my love for horses, I don't know how my life would have turned out. I had friends then, other kids my age who were also working students and loved horses. The horses were our bond, and we spent endless hours talking about horses, riding together, and working side by side. That was during my formative years, from twelve through my late teens. I am very lucky to have had that, because otherwise I would have been a lonely and bored teen, because I had no friends at school.

In the midnineties I got interested in military aviation after watching the movie *Top Gun*. I decided I wanted to fly in a fighter jet, a seemingly impossible feat for a civilian, and that was all there was to it. This was, by far, the most bizarre fixation I ever got. I moved from Wisconsin to Pensacola, Florida, to chase my dream.

Still employed full-time as an anesthetist, I spent the next seven years working toward my goal. I became an internationally published military aviation photojournalist and wrote freelance articles for magazines like *Wings of Gold, Naval Aviation News, Air Sports International, Combat Aircraft*, and more. On December 6, 2002, in the backseat of an F-15 at Eglin Air Force base, I realized my dream. I sat there, in literal disbelief that I was really there, in that mighty fighter jet, going down the runway in a full afterburner takeoff, then climbing straight up to 15,000 feet for the flight of a lifetime.

Two months after my F-15 flight, I was writing an article about a helicopter training squadron at Naval Air Station Whiting Field in Milton, Florida, and they gave me a one and a half hour flight in a TH-57 Sea Ranger helicopter. I got to sit in the student seat and actually take the controls. I had spent several hours the day before in a helicopter simulator with a flight instructor.

Ice dancing became another one of my fixations. I practiced at 4 a.m. before my college classes, and got a job as a skate guard at the arena. Working at the arena enabled me to get free ice time when the arena was closed to the public. I skated from 1977 to 1983. In 1982, while in my last year at Bloomfield College, I fell and broke my left arm during a practice session. While I was in the emergency room, an anesthesiologist came in to sedate me before the orthopedic surgeon set my arm. During the procedure, the anesthesiologist asked me a question that would direct me down another path. I mentioned that I was a student, and he inquired what I was studying. I replied, "Nursing. Getting my BSN." He asked why I didn't go on to be a CRNA, a certified registered nurse anesthetist. So right then and there, with my arm in a cast, I found my lifelong career.

My passion for animals was apparently present at birth. I have an exceptional communication with all animals, and I can figure out what they are doing and why they are doing it. I feel fortunate to have this unusual ability. Animals are extremely special to me, providing me peace and comfort. Let me apologize ahead of time for the lengthy chapter about all of my animals. I felt it necessary to write a great deal about them, because they are all such an important aspect of my life.

After finding out I had Asperger's syndrome, I became obsessed with learning everything I could about it. Now my new special interest is to become an advocate for others with Asperger's syndrome. I have started a support group in my community for people with Asperger's, which has become a rewarding experience.

Research has shown that people with autism and Asperger's have extremely low levels of oxytocin. Oxytocin is known as the bonding hormone, and it is produced naturally by the body. Since oxytocin plays a key role in a person's ability to socially interact, this could be a major factor in a person with Asperger's not being able to make friends and having such difficulty socializing with people. I wonder if it also explains why people shun those with Asperger's, because they somehow sense the lack of bonding ability. Parents of an Asperger's child often notice that when their child goes to interact with children their own age, their child is shunned. I've wondered about that, and after reading all this research, I feel that somehow other people can sense this low level of oxytocin in people with autism and Asperger's syndrome.

I want to emphasize that everything I have accomplished in my life was a struggle, because I had to work hard to compensate for my social limitations. I have not overcome them, but I developed coping mechanisms. Having ridicule and humiliation directed at me became a normal way of life. It was not that I accepted it. I simply realized that some people need to do this to people they perceive as lesser than themselves. But I knew that just because someone is different does not mean she is less. From my experiences, I have developed great compassion for anyone who is different, in whatever way that might be. I believe we (the different) all have a unique bond.

I have maintained a positive attitude throughout my life, and I want to motivate others to do the same. I want to inspire them and assure them that no matter what life hands you, happiness and a productive life can be yours. Whatever your beginnings, no matter how humble or difficult, if you stay focused and follow your heart and your dreams, you will eventually reach your goal. Be proud that you are different.

Asperger's syndrome does have some negative aspects to it, but it also has some extremely positive ones. I will show you what focusing on those positive aspects can achieve. I was handed lemons, but I made lemonade. You can too!

Anita Lesko

What Is Asperger's Syndrome?

The following information is from WebMD.com. It provides a concise discussion of what Asperger's syndrome is and identifies the main symptom as severe trouble with social situations.

Symptoms during childhood:

Parents may not notice a problem with their child until preschool, when they begin to interact with other children. At that point the child may:

1. not pick up on social cues and not be able to read others' body language, or start and maintain a conversation;
2. exhibit strong attachment to routine;
3. exhibit strong aversion to a change or break in routine;
4. appear to lack empathy;
5. be unable to recognize subtle differences in speech tone, pitch, and accent that alter the meaning of others' speech. Thus the child may not understand a joke or may take a sarcastic comment literally. Likewise, the child may have speech that is flat and difficult to understand because it lacks tone, pitch, and accent;
6. speak at an advanced level for their age;
7. avoid eye contact;
8. have unusual facial expressions or postures;

9. be preoccupied with only one or a few special interests, which they may be very knowledgeable about;

10. talk a lot, usually about a favorite subject. One-sided conversations are common;

11. have delayed motor development. The child may be late in learning to use a fork or spoon, ride a bike, or catch a ball. They may have an awkward walk. Handwriting is often poor;

12. have heightened sensitivity and become overstimulated by loud noises, lights, smells, tastes, or textures.

A child with one or two of these symptoms does not necessarily have Asperger's syndrome. To be diagnosed with Asperger's, a child must have a combination of these symptoms and severe trouble with social situations.

As the child enters her teen years, she will want friends but will continue having social difficulties. She will feel different from others. Although most teens place emphasis on being and looking "cool," teens with Asperger's may find it frustrating and emotionally draining to try to fit in. They may be immature for their age, as well as naïve and too trusting, which can lead to teasing and bullying.

Asperger's syndrome is a lifelong condition, although it tends to stabilize over time. Adults usually obtain a better understanding of their own strengths and weaknesses. Socializing improves, as they are able to learn social skills and how to read others' social cues.

Some traits that are typical of Asperger's syndrome, such as attention to detail and focused interests, can increase chances of university and career success. Many people with Asperger's are of high intelligence. Among the many famous people who might have had Asperger's are Albert Einstein, Wolfgang Amadeus Mozart, Thomas Jefferson, and some of the great inventors of our time.

Studies indicate that as many as three to four children out of every thousand have Asperger's syndrome. It affects boys more often than girls. Research also suggests that Asperger's syndrome has a genetic component.

Formal diagnosis consists of a series of tests administered by a psychologist or psychiatrist, including an IQ test, along with lengthy interviews of the individual.

History of Asperger's Syndrome.

As noted in Wikipedia, Asperger's syndrome, an autism spectrum disorder, is a relatively new diagnosis in the field of autism. It was named for Hans Asperger (1906–80), an Austrian psychiatrist and pediatrician. Asperger exhibited many of the features of the condition named after him. Asperger believed children with Asperger's syndrome would be capable of exceptional achievement and original thought later in life.

Chapter 1:

———◆———

Born Different: Starting Out in Life with Asperger's Syndrome

I have an excellent memory and can remember back to when I was quite young, as early as four years old. There were three kids who I knew literally from birth, Candy, Bobby, and Allison. They were the children of my mom's best friend, and we all played together on a regular basis. These were the only kids I had any contact with prior to kindergarten. We got along well, but I remember playing alongside them more than with them. I preferred sitting with my mom and her friend Sara to being with the kids. But when I was with them it was peaceful.

Early Childhood

When I was about four and a half, I began the long journey of experiencing life as "different," and not fitting in. My mom took me to a nearby playground, and I can see it very clearly, my excitement as I walked down the little hill toward the swings and merry-go-round. For whatever reason, I was drawn to the merry-go-round, which a number of children were playing on. As I neared the ride, the other kids took one look at me and ran away. At the time I was glad that I now had the merry-go-round to myself. I didn't care that the kids ran away from me. I became obsessed with making the merry-go-round spin around and around, the faster the better. That was all I wanted to do. I was having a wonderful time, not knowing my mom was watching and crying. She was crying because she saw how the other children reacted to me when I approached them. She saw them all look at me as if I were from another planet and wondered what she had done wrong in raising me. Little did she know she'd be wondering that for the next forty-nine years, always blaming herself that I was so different and didn't fit in.

It didn't matter what playground I was taken to, the same thing happened again and again. I'd no sooner walk over to wherever other children were, and they would look at me and leave. Several years ago someone told me that if you fill a bowl with water and shake pepper all over the water, then get a piece of soap and hold it in the center of the water, the pepper instantly disperses away from the soap. I conducted the experiment in my kitchen, and the first thing that came to my mind was that that was what it was like to be me. I didn't know at the time that I had Asperger's. Try this little experiment yourself, and then try to imagine what it's like to have Asperger's syndrome, and that all that pepper is people fleeing from you.

I dreaded the prospect of starting kindergarten, knowing there would be lots of kids and lots of noise. As a young child, I thrived on peace and quiet, and was happy to be around adults. I was most upset knowing that I had to go in there myself, without my mother. That first day was a nightmare to me, and it pretty much didn't change throughout the next thirteen years, until I graduated from high school. It was, simply put, a torture chamber for me. The external stimuli was overwhelming, from the noise—children playing, teachers talking, bells ringing—the strange smells, getting bullied, forced to do things against my will, and being away from the security of home.

Mom holding me at 5 months old

Reading at a High Level

By the time I was four, I was reading at a high school level. I loved to read, but only what I wanted to read. One time when my mom took me to the doctor for a regular checkup, she brought along a book I was reading, so I could show him how I could read. The doctor was puzzled, and stated he'd never seen anything like it before. Once in school, I had absolutely no interest in reading the things expected of us, like "See Spot's spot." *You've got to be kidding me,* I'd think. What a waste of my time to read about Dick and

Jane. Later in life, I nearly didn't get accepted into Bloomfield College's nursing program, because I failed the reading section of their entrance exam. Apparently I got a zero on it. The chairperson of the nursing program told me during my interview that normally they wouldn't accept someone with a failure in reading, but she had a feeling there was something special about me. She made an exception and accepted me into their program. I've thought of her many times, because if it weren't for her, I don't know where I'd be.

Feeling Anxious

I recently found my kindergarten report card. My teacher had written that I appeared anxious all the time, and never seemed to calm down. That teacher obviously read me well, because I was always anxious, and irritated too. One thing that really bugged me was the rest period each day, when we were to take out our mat from our cubbyhole, place it on the floor, and take a nap. Each time I had to do that, I'd lie down and look at the other kids lying on their mats, and I would think that it was senseless to be wasting time like this. I just wanted it to be over. I also didn't like lying down amid all those kids. The teacher would scold me to close my eyes and go to sleep. I never could. I just wanted out of school, and that naptime was simply another delay. I'm sure the look on my face was one of disgust and annoyance. This obviously irritated the teacher, because she repeatedly called my mother in to discuss my noncompliance with the rules. She would say to my mother that I wasn't like the other children, I wouldn't listen to her, and I wasn't fitting in with everyone else. I just seemed to do what I wanted to, and was in my own little world.

Another thing I came to dread was the school bell, which rang every hour to signal something. The first time I heard it, I nearly fainted. After figuring out the times it would ring, I'd look at the clock and try to prepare myself to hear that shrill, harsh, nightmare sound. Of course it didn't bother anyone else, something I readily observed. What was wrong with them? I wondered. How could they be oblivious to that horrible sound?

At first my mother thought I was stubborn, but eventually realized that I was strong-willed, a trait that would help me overcome the many obstacles I faced throughout my life. Perseverance was another trait I'd been born with, which would help me out along the way. The one thing that neither my mother nor I knew was that I had Asperger's syndrome, which would affect every aspect of my life, and my interactions with all the people I met.

Daydreaming in School When I Should Have Been Paying Attention

First grade was even worse. The teacher expected students to pay attention to her droning on about worthless information. I simply couldn't see the point of anything she had to say. I had much more interesting things to do, like gaze out the window at the lush green grass and imagine myself galloping along on a beautiful white horse. I could hear the wind blowing past my ears and the hoofbeats pounding the earth; feel the power beneath me as the thick mane flowed back. This wonderful illusion was frequently interrupted by the teacher calling out my name. Several times. Finally I'd hear it. I would look at her and she'd repeat her question. Of course I didn't know the answer, because I hadn't been paying attention and had no idea what she had been talking about. The teacher would get mad and all the kids would laugh at me. It would bother me a little, but not enough to stop my vivid daydreaming and start paying attention in class instead. Naturally, my mother was called in to see the teacher, and eventually the principal as well. In fact, my mother would become a regular visitor to Mr. D's office.

Realizing I Was Different

I would often watch other kids playing with one another and wonder why they never wanted to play with me. I had absolutely no clue how to relate to people my own age. Eventually I realized that I was content to be by myself and do my own entertaining. I wasn't much interested in what the other kids were doing anyway. If I did make an effort to try to play with the kids, they would shun me and I'd feel sad. It was a lot nicer for me not to even try to interact with my peers. Perhaps it was a way of self-preservation.

Bullying Victim

Of course, there was the never-ending bullying. Bullies called me names, shoved me, poked me, anything to harass me. Lots of people are bullied when they are young, for many reasons. I'm not going to bore you with everything I went through, except for a few highlights, like the apple story. I will, however, elaborate on being bullied in the workplace later in the book, because that can threaten your livelihood. As I came to learn, workplace bullying is the worst kind there is.

It was the summer between third and fourth grade when I learned just how mean your peers can be. In our front yard was a big apple tree that produced tons of apples each year. In our side yard was a small pool, probably two feet deep and ten feet in diameter. It was a hot day at the end of the summer, and I was in the pool—by myself of course—just sitting there enjoying the relief from the heat. Meanwhile, four neighborhood boys knocked on our front door and asked my mom if they could pick apples from our tree. My mom said yes, and even gave them a basket to collect the fruit in. Patrick and his three friends were fourteen; I was nine. My mother had returned to reading her book outside when she heard me screaming. She came racing over to the pool to find Patrick and his friends pelting me with the apples they had just picked. In less than a couple of minutes I had been hit with dozens of our own apples. The incident left me with a bloody nose, a split lip that needed several stitches, two black eyes, and emotional trauma.

Being different is like wearing a sign that says Bully Me. I'm convinced there is such a sign on me, because bullies can always find me.

Learning to Enjoy the Beauty of Nature

Despite all the unpleasantness I suffered each day at school, when I wasn't there I actually was a happy person. My mom would take me for walks on a regular basis, and that was always fun. My deep love of nature began on those many walks. We'd be walking along on a crisp fall morning, and I would be enjoying the fresh air, the vapor coming out of my mouth upon exhalation, the sound of the fallen leaves crunching beneath our feet—and then we'd stop so Mom could pick up a beautiful leaf off the ground. She would point out the veins on the back to show the complex beauty of nature. We'd look at the leaf's stunning orange color, examine its texture. Then we would look at the tree the leaf had fallen from, and admire the hundreds of bright leaves remaining on the tree, and how striking it looked standing next to a tree that had all deep red leaves. Dawn became one of my most favorite events in the fall and winter, as I watched the color palate change from light grays to peach to lavender, and all the cloud formations. Once while walking to school one morning, Mom said to stop. It had snowed the night before, and the sun shone on the snow, creating an effect of millions of diamonds glittering across the snow-covered fields. Other people were just walking along, none of them stopping to drink in the beauty of nature. I felt so rich that I was able to get so much out of that beauty. I'm still like that today. I feel very lucky that I am able to get so much joy and happiness from nature. Most people never see it. They're too busy talking on cell phones, texting, tweeting, just going through the motions of life.

My mother enjoyed the writings of Henry David Thoreau, a naturalist, in particular his book *Walden*, a reflection upon simple living in natural surroundings. She would talk about her readings to me on our walks to and from school. I was particularly struck by one of Thoreau's most famous sayings:

"If a man does not keep pace with his companions, perhaps it is because he hears a different drummer. Let him step to the music which he hears, however measured or far away."

The instant I heard this, I knew it was written for me. I was indeed marching to my own drummer, which was apparently very far away from my peers.

Me age one and a half, and me age 2 at Christmas

Valentine's Day: Knowing I Wasn't Going to Get Any Cards

I was in third grade at the time. Since the teachers knew my mother was a skilled artist, on the holidays they always asked her to make something for the classroom. This time it was a request for a big box decorated for Valentine's Day, for the kids to put their cards for one another in the box. Mom went all out, decorating a huge box, the size of one from a TV. She spent days on it, even trimming it with beautiful lace. I remember her bringing it to my classroom and setting it up on the front table. Everyone was excited, including the teacher, who praised my mom for all her hard work. This was two weeks before Valentine's Day. On the day itself, students would put their cards in the box, we'd have a big party, and then the cards would be handed out. There was only one very big problem.

As I sat in class each day and admired my mom's handiwork, the realization set in that there were not going to be any cards in that entire box for me. Not even one. It was going to be very embarrassing to be the only kid in the class without even one card. I came up with the perfect solution to this problem. My mom had bought me a box of Valentine cards to give to each kid in my class. My secret plan was to write them all out to myself, using different handwriting for each one. No one would ever suspect! So, I proceeded with my plan and wrote out each card to myself. I sneaked the cards into that box over several days, using great caution that no one saw me put them in there. Once the cards were successfully housed in the box, I felt quite smug, knowing I would receive thirty-five cards on Valentine's Day.

Finally the big day arrived. The teacher had gone all out decorating the classroom with all sorts of Valentine decorations. The big card box was the focal point of the room, ready to be opened and the cards distributed. Two students were assigned to hand out the cards. As they delivered the cards to all the students, I sat and watched my pile of cards growing on my desk. I felt so proud to be like everyone else and get lots of cards. When it was all done, the card-giving turned out just as I'd suspected. Other than the cards I sent to myself, there were no other cards. I was thankful I had dreamed up my scheme, because I would have wanted to crawl under a rock and hide, rather than sit there with an empty desktop. As everyone opened their cards, I looked around the room and thought how lonely I felt at that moment. The consequences of being different and not fitting in were starting to sink in. The realization was overwhelming.

I thought I was going to fool even my mom with my big collection of Valentine cards. Once at home, I took them all out to show her. She never let on that she figured out exactly what I had done. Nor did I know that she cried herself to sleep that night over the whole thing. It wasn't until years later that she told me that she knew what I had pulled off. She still tells me that it was worse for her to see all the horrible things that happened to me, than it was for me, the person who was actually experiencing the events.

> ## Power Point
>
> **My advice to educators is, for any holiday, emphasize to all the children that a card or small gift must be given to *each* of the students, and it is the teacher's responsibility to check what each student has to give out, to ensure that there is one for each child. What I described above is guaranteed to happen to at least one child in your class, whether they have AS or for some other reason. You can prevent it by taking the simple steps I described. Thank you.**

The School System Didn't Know What to Do with Me

How I ever made it out of elementary school is a mystery to me. The teachers and administrators simply didn't know what to do with me. They would admit to my mom that they recognized that I was exceptionally bright, but that I could not, or would not, be part of the class and participate like everyone else. One crazy thing that I couldn't seem to master was filling out a test sheet properly. On multiple-choice exams, for example, I couldn't get the hang of filling in the corresponding little circle for the correct answer. One test I remember in particular, the answer sheet was a light pine green. For each numbered questions, there were five corresponding circles labeled a, b, c, d, and e. Those were the answer choices. Instead of choosing an answer for question one and then going on to the next question, I filled in all the circles for each question. Obviously I flunked the test spectacularly. No one could explain to me how to do it correctly. My brain literally shut down. The principal even had me come to his office so he could try to explain it to me. I clearly remember sitting right next to Mr. D and hearing him drone on about how to do it. I kept staring down at that green paper with my brain totally blank. It seemed I sat there for an eternity with him. I just wanted to go home.

About a week later a teacher came into my classroom and called my name to come with her. I silently went along, walking down the empty halls. We came to a door. She opened it, led me inside to a desk, and ordered me to stay there. No pencil, no books, no paper, just sit there. After she walked out, I slowly looked around the room. There was a teacher, or at least someone who looked like a teacher, sitting at the front of the room reading a book. She seemed oblivious to anything in the room. I became concerned as I continued my survey of the room. All of the other kids in there were in wheelchairs, their heads tilted to the side, drool coming out of their mouths. I was totally bewildered as to why I'd been brought to this room. I stayed there until the last bell rang at the end of the day. The second I saw my mom, I told her all about what had happened. Although Mom never said anything to me, I knew she was in a rage over it. The next morning she was at the school the second it opened and made a beeline for the principal's office. I heard a lot of yelling going on behind that door, but the only thing I know is that I was never taken to that room again.

Mom 1960

Uncoordinated

My total lack of coordination tormented me. I couldn't learn to tie shoelaces, so Mom had to find me shoes that just slipped on. I couldn't catch a ball, not even a huge medicine ball. Not even in high school. I can remember a high-school girl, one of the in-crowd girls, throwing that medicine ball at me with all her might. It hit me right in the face, knocking me onto my back. The laughter that ensued still echoes in my head. In kindergarten when we had exercise time, the teachers would take us outside to run around a big field to warm up. I could hardly walk without tripping, so I dreaded running. I couldn't keep up with the other kids, because of my tripping and awkward running. Just another avenue of mockery. I couldn't get the hang of much of any games, like jumping rope or hopscotch, anything that involved coordination.

Handwriting was another matter that plagued me. I could print very fast without giving it a second thought. Handwriting, however, necessitated me concentrating on every letter I wrote, which greatly slowed my ability to take notes in class or write essays for tests that had time limits. I was a mystery to everyone.

Sensitive to Touch

Another battle I fought daily was my sensitivity to touch, especially of certain fabrics, and my absolute intolerance of socks. My mother would no sooner put socks on my feet than I'd be pulling them off. She says I was about three years old when I started doing that. Clothing was another issue that drove Mom nuts. I couldn't stand any fabrics that were scratchy or had any kind of rough feeling. And I couldn't wear anything that was tight. I couldn't even stand to see tight clothes on someone else, or see scratchy fabrics. I'm still like that now. In the operating room I wear scrubs, of course, and they're two sizes too big. Wearing them for as long as fourteen hours straight necessitates that comfort. I literally cringe when I see coworkers in tight scrubs that look like they are ready to pop. Even seeing someone tying his shoes very tight discomfits me.

Teachers Try to Force Me to Tumble

Another elementary school nightmare was gym class, especially when we started gymnastics. As uncoordinated as I was, I still liked the balance beam and the other equipment. However, I was terrified of tumbling. All the other students took to it like a duck to water, but there was simply no way I was going to do it. Absolutely not. You were supposed to put your feet pretty far apart, lean forward, place your palms on the mat, tuck your head between your legs, squat down, and tumble over. For whatever reason, I was just terrified to do it. After I spent some time telling the four gym teachers that I wasn't going to do it, the next thing I know, I was surrounded by the four teachers. They each took hold of me. One foot got pulled one way, the other foot pulled the other way. They grabbed my arms and put my hands on the floor, and then shoved my head down toward my chest. They all started trying to push me over. From somewhere within me came the strength of a raging bull. I pushed the whole lot of them off me and ran out of the gymnasium. Of course my mother was called in to the principal's office. I'm sure it wasn't pretty what mom had to say to him. In this day and age, a parent could sue a school if teachers tried to physically force a child to do something like that. The good news was, they never did it again to me.

Power Point

Do not ever force an AS child to do something like this, or any child for that matter. It is overwhelmingly traumatic for the child.

Coming to Life When I Started Taking Riding Lessons

I was in fifth grade when I began horse-riding lessons. In the chapter The Purple and Orange Witch, I elaborate on my passion for horses, but the following pertains specifically to elementary school.

I couldn't learn to jump rope, or do much of anything physical, because I was so uncoordinated. Teachers regularly sent messages to my mom about my plight, and I almost didn't graduate from high school because of a failing mark in physical education. But a very peculiar thing happened when I went for my first horse-riding lesson. The uncoordinated kid suddenly was coordinated. I think it was because I *wanted* to be coordinated! I apparently was a natural-born rider. A group lesson started in early October, and I wanted desperately to sign up for the ten-week session. However, the lessons started at 3:30 each Friday. Students were supposed to arrive at 3 p.m. to help get their horses ready. I didn't get out of school until 3, and the stable was a good half hour away. My mother wrote a letter to the principal, requesting that for ten weeks I be excused from school at 2:00 on Fridays so I could attend the riding lessons. Oddly enough, the request was approved! I suspect the school was so desperate for me to be able to do *something*, it was worth it to let me out that hour earlier for ten weeks.

I vividly remember the first Friday that I was going to leave school early. That morning I took my riding boots to school in a bag, to put on before I left the building. In my last class, I was hyperventilating with excitement, watching the clock and counting the seconds until it was 2:00. Of course, I wasn't paying any attention to what the rest of the class or the teacher was doing. I was wondering what kind of horse I would get for the lesson. About ten minutes before two, my teacher looked over at me and nodded that I was allowed to leave. I grabbed my bag with the boots in it and rapidly exited the classroom. In the girl's room, I put my boots on. I was beside myself as I took off my shoes and pulled those shiny new boots on with the boot pulls. I'd bought the boots with money I'd saved up from doing odd jobs for my mom. I loved the smell of new leather.

I ran out of the school. My mom was waiting for me in the car outside the front door. I jumped in and slammed the door. She knew I was ready to explode with excitement. We talked all the way to the stable. The best part of the trip to the stable was driving through Eagle Rock Reservation. It's similar to driving through the Black Forest in Germany, up a narrow, winding road, going higher and higher, the sun flickering between the thick trees. At the top of the mountain is a lookout area from where you can see the New York City skyline. It is quite spectacular.

Mom pulled up in front of the stable, and the car was not even stopped before I was climbing out and heading to the front door. I checked in at their office, and then headed through the main barn to the stairs. The stairs led down to the school barn, where all the school horses were stabled. As I walked through the main barn, I looked with envy at the privately owned horses in their stalls, munching away on their hay. *Someday,* I thought, *someday I'll own my own horse.* I proceeded down the stairs and went to the office to find out what horse I'd be riding that day. In the office was a girl in her early twenties with a clipboard in her hand, and several people standing around her. She asked me who I was, and then told me I was to ride Ghost, the black horse with the white head. Ghost had albino eyes to go with his white head. I thought he was the ugliest horse I'd ever seen. Many years later, while I was watching TV with my mom, an ad came on for a big department store. In the ad people were riding horses, and one of the horses was Ghost! I got so excited, and I said to Mom, "There's Ghost!" She said it wasn't very probable, but I said there couldn't be another horse that ugly. Several months later, by chance I ran into someone I'd know during my riding days and mentioned seeing Ghost. She laughed and confirmed that, yes indeed, it was Ghost. He had been bought by a lady who worked in advertising at that department store, and she had had that ad made specifically so her beloved horse could be on TV. I marveled that anyone would want that ugly horse on television. I doubt even Ghost's mother thought he was nice looking.

So back to school I went on Monday. No one asked me anything about my riding lesson, and I certainly didn't talk to anyone about it. I think it was worked out so that no students knew why I was leaving school early on those days. Fine with me. I didn't have any friends, and the other kids liked me about as much as I liked them. I went through the motions and somehow made it out of sixth grade. I hated every minute of those school years, every single aspect of them. I thought everything was a waste of time, and that what they taught was totally worthless. I hated being around my peers, because when they weren't shunning me, they were bullying me. So what was there to like about it? Nothing. I didn't fit in, and I knew it. The thought of attending high school terrified me. I knew the bullying was going to be worse there.

On my last day of sixth grade, my mom took me out to eat after the little graduation ceremony. During our lunch she started talking about high school and how she knew it was going to be horrible for me, but I was going to need to start preparing myself for what lay ahead. She explained that if I ever really wanted to own a horse, I was going to need a good education, and I would need to study hard to get that. That was all she needed to say to me to lift my spirits and give me the confidence to face high school. Her words stayed in my mind from that day forward.

Power Point

When your AS child finds something he or she loves, encourage him and do whatever it takes to enable him to do it. Whether it eventually turns into a career for him or is just a passion, it will be a bonus for his well-being.

The Hardships of Growing Up Poor

My biological father was a surgeon who left when I was two years old. Neither my mother nor I ever saw him again or had any contact with him. About two years ago

I decided to try and search for him, at which time I discovered he died in 1989. I was able to obtain his death certificate from the Florida Bureau of Records, and saw he died of cardiac arrest secondary to lung cancer. He had only one other child, a son, who became a physician as well. I have never met this half brother, but I'm quite sure he has Asperger's Syndrome. He is a world-renowned researcher with multiple patents on a number of specific drugs, which are used worldwide for a very high-profile disease. He obviously has a laser focus to have accomplished all of that.

Regarding my other half brother whom I discuss in chapter 12, for reasons too lengthy to explain here we were not raised together. He is nine years older than me and was raised by my mother's parents in Pennsylvania.

My father who raised me did not participate in my life, and was never present at any major milestones. It was always just me and Mom. So from here on when I refer to my parents, this is the father aspect.

My parents were very poor, so I didn't have much when growing up. My mom had to make all of our clothing, and food was always from scratch. She'd have me in the kitchen watching her from the beginning, and then I started helping her with small tasks. Eventually, I was right next to her making rustic, old-world breads, kneading the dough, and making an endless array of other foods. That's where my love of cooking and baking came from. At one point in my life I contemplated becoming a chef. Now I'm just a chef at home, and I find great peace and comfort working away in the kitchen, cooking up some elaborate dinner. I never had any interest in sewing, so Mom didn't have any luck trying to recruit my help when she was working on clothing. Her clothes were so beautifully made, they could have been made by a professional, but they were different. Yet another way for me to stand out!

We had a wringer washer that Mom used for washing clothes, and our little house on Woodland Road was heated by a coal furnace. A fire had to be maintained in the furnace in the cellar at all times. If it went out, it was quite the production to get it started again. My mom has been sickly her whole life, and had pneumonia seven times. One particular time, it was the middle of January, and I was seven years old. Very sick with pneumonia, Mom also had a high fever. It was below freezing outside, and it was snowing. The furnace went out, and it started to get very cold in the house. My mom coughed and coughed, sounding and looking very weak. She got out of bed and slowly made her way down into the cellar to relight the fire. I wanted to help her, but she never wanted me near that furnace. I stayed at the top of the cellar stairs and peered down at her, struggling to get a fire going. She had to keep sitting down on a rocking chair to rest. Finally, after a huge fire was roaring away in the furnace, she went back upstairs to her bed, climbed in, and covered herself with several blankets. I could see she had the chills real bad, and I was so worried about her. I sat there crying quietly so she wouldn't hear me. I didn't want to get her any more upset than she already was.

My grandparents on my mother's side came to America from Czechoslovakia. I remember them telling their tales about arriving at Ellis Island and signing in there, and literally having no money in their pockets. They ended up in Wilkes-Barre, Pennsylvania, and stayed there the rest of their lives. My grandfather started work as a coal miner when he was nine, and worked there until he was sixty. He died at the age of sixty-five from black lung, as did so many miners after working in the mines their whole lives.

Wanting to Play with Plastic Horses Instead of Dolls

I never liked to play with dolls, I preferred plastic horses. I had a whole collection of western horses as well as Johnny West, the western rider that went with them. I could play for hours with them. The other thing I'd do for entertainment was set up an obstacle course in the backyard to jump over, and I would pretend I was jumping a horse over them, even galloping around the course.

> ## Power Point
>
> To parents—Don't insist that your daughter play with Barbie dolls. If you want to have them for yourself, that's fine, but let your child play with whatever she wants. My mother tried giving me dolls, and I'd throw them aside and go back to playing with the horses. I've talked to a number of AS women who told me they didn't like dolls either. One played with horses like me, and some of the others wanted GI Joe dolls.

Savoring the Solitude of the Beaches of Cape May, New Jersey

Once a year my mom and I ventured down to Cape May, the southernmost point in New Jersey. I loved to walk on the beach, alone. Mom would sit on a blanket on the sand, and I'd never go out of her sight. But just walking along the water's edge, feeling the little waves come in over my feet and hearing the wind blow past my ears, was very peaceful. I haven't been to Cape May for probably thirty years, but back then it was very quiet, nothing commercial, and the beaches would be totally empty by 5 p.m. It was like having your own private beach. My most favorite spot on the boardwalk was Morrow's Nut House. I can still smell the incredible aromas that would waft in the air as you opened the door. There were all kinds of candies—salt water taffy, fudge, cotton candy, those red candy apples that crackle when you bite into them, and all sorts of roasted nuts. All those fragrances melding together made for a sensory delight like no other. I'd get my vanilla walnut fudge in a little white box, and we'd go sit outside by the jetty and watch the waves of the Atlantic Ocean come crashing in. Plenty of times we got sprayed by the big ones.

Me on Sunset Beach in Cape May New Jersey in my early years

I Don't Want to Attend My Birthday Party

The last emotionally distressing event I'll share from my childhood is my Asperger's birthday party, as I call it. McDonald's had a contest. The winner received burgers, fries, and drinks for twenty-five people for a birthday party. We were notified that I had won; and as it happened, my birthday was just weeks away. My mom invited the requisite twenty-five people, some adults but mostly kids from my class and neighbors. She lavishly decorated a room in our house, and had someone pick up the huge order from McDonald's. Everyone was milling about waiting for the goodies to arrive. Everyone, that is, except me. I was nowhere to be found. Mom went through the house looking for me. She finally found me sitting on the stairs, crying. I wanted no part of being with all those people and the chaos and noise. I simply wouldn't budge. So there I sat and cried throughout the entire party. I ate my burgers and fries after everyone was gone. No one could figure out why I did that, but now we know why. So it's pretty funny thinking back on it.

A Ruptured Appendix at Age Seven

When I was seven, I spent nearly two weeks in the pediatric intensive care unit. It was the middle of winter, and everyone was getting the flu. I started getting sick, and then I was very sick. My mother called the pediatrician's office to make an appointment to bring me in. The nurse told her they were booked solid, and I probably had the flu like everyone else. The nurse told her some things to do to expedite my recovery. Mom had an uneasy feeling, and shortly thereafter called the nurse back. My mom told her she thought something was really wrong with me and that I looked strange. She insisted on talking to the doctor. The nurse got him on the phone, but he was extremely annoyed that she had bothered him, stating that every kid in town had the flu.

After she got off the phone with the doctor, I looked even worse. Mom called the neighbor across the street, Monique, to ask her to take us to the hospital. I was bundled up and off we went, At the emergency room, they quickly did some blood work and then called in a surgeon. I had a ruptured appendix, and I was rushed up to the operating room. My mother was a basket case, and I was scared but quiet.

I was quickly prepped for surgery. Two staff people came to get me for the long ride on the gurney to the OR. It was 11 p.m. I have a vivid memory of lying on that gurney, going down a dimly lit hallway, looking at windows that looked out into the darkness. As the gurney slowed down to turn into the OR, I started crying. I stared around the huge room, all the people in funny clothes, the big, bright lights above the operating table, and all of the instruments. I was really scared now. Suddenly one of the nurses that was pushing my gurney pinched me hard, all over my body, saying sternly, "Shut up, kid. Shut up, kid." They lifted me onto the operating table, with those bright lights glaring in my eyes, and then a black rubber mask was slammed onto my face. A nauseating smell filled the mask. Everything got blurred and wavy.

The next thing I knew I awoke in the pediatric intensive care unit, my mother sitting next to the bed holding my hand. It was 3:30 a.m. I had IVs in each hand and one in my foot. There were lots of funny machines next to the bed. I felt very tired. They had told Mom that because my appendix had ruptured, peritonitis had already set in. I had nearly died, and would need the IV antibiotics for two weeks. I told my mom about the nurse pinching me. She reported it to the surgeon. He came to examine me and found bruises all over my body. The nurse was fired later that day.

The best part of my hospital stay was that Mom brought me lots of presents, something exciting each day. My favorite was a pretend milkshake. It was a pretty pink glass, like an old-fashioned Coke glass, with a white metal holder around the base. White carnations filled the top, looking like whipped cream, with a straw sticking out and a cherry on top. Once I got back home, I remained out of school for the next two months. That was awesome. No bullying, no torment for two whole months. It was worth all the pain to get that.

A Very Large Head for My Age

My mother noticed early on that my head was abnormally large for my body, and compared to other kids my age. When I started to ride horses, before I was even allowed on one, Mom took me to get a riding helmet. We went to a local horse supply store that sold everything from horse feed to saddles to riding apparel. The lady brought out several helmets and handed me one to try on. It wouldn't even go beyond being perched on top of my head. The lady looked puzzled. She took all the helmets back and returned with a few more. After trying them all, I ended up with the largest adult size available. With the huge helmet on, I truly looked like a space alien. I appeared in danger of toppling over from the weight on my head.

In her book, *The Way I See It*, Temple Grandin discusses detecting babies at risk for developing autism and Asperger's by taking their head measurements.[1] According

---

1   Temple Grandin, *The Way I See It: A Personal Look at Autism and Asperger's* (Texas: Future Horizons, 2008), 195.

to Dr. Courchesne and his colleagues at the School of Medicine, University of California, it may be possible to identify babies at risk for developing autism spectrum disorders by measuring the size of their heads. He states brain overgrowth occurs before the onset of obviously abnormal behaviors. There is as much as 20 percent enlargement.

Chapter 2:

Surviving the Teen Years with My Invisible Disorder

I dreaded starting junior high school. A family had moved onto our street with a teenage daughter, my age, who immediately started bullying me. She seemed to pull together a neighborhood gang overnight to strengthen her bullying powers. Terri was huge for her age, had a big mop of black frizzy hair, and pimples all over her face. Just the sight of her frightened me.

The end of my first week of seventh grade, something happened that scares me to this day. My mom was waiting to pick me up at 3 p.m., and she saw me walking down the driveway of the school. I had to cross a pedestrian bridge over a river to get to the parking area. I didn't realize Terri and her gang were closing in behind me. Just as I started across the bridge, Terri shoved me against the stone wall, which was about three feet high. Out of the corner of my eye I could see the water flowing below. I'm terrified of water and cannot swim, and I knew that river was over ten feet deep. Terri and her gang screamed names at me and kept shoving me like they were going to push me over the side. My mom had jumped out of the car and was running toward us. The kids were yelling that they were going to shove me into the river, when Terri looked in the direction of someone who was shouting, "Stop! Stop!" It was my mother, and Terri knew that. She let me go and started running away, her gang in tow. I was crying by this point, and shaking so badly I could hardly stand.

Home wasn't the next stop; the Bloomfield police station was. My mom filed complaints on Terri and her buddies. She demanded that the police put a stop to their bullying, and she wasn't going to waste her time going to the school about it. By the next morning the police had contacted all of the kids' parents and ordered them and the kids to come to the station. They were informed that if anything like that ever happened again, juvenile criminal charges would be filed and the kids would be expelled from school. Those parents must have heard that loud and clear, because Terri and her gang didn't so much as look at me again.

My Sensory Overload through Crowded School Hallways

My biggest recollection of junior high and high school was the sensory overload, from the bell ringing at the conclusion of each class, and then the subsequent migration to the next class amid an ocean of people surging through the hallways. I constantly wondered why all this bothered me so much, because it was apparent that others were oblivious to it. Even the smells got to me. Lots of people used perfumes and colognes, adding to the magnitude of this event, which occurred eight times a day, Monday through Friday. I had no friends in junior high or high school. The few friends I had were at the riding stable. I got bullied in the usual fashion, which I had become used to: being called names, laughed at, and the several girls who thought it was their duty to try to push me down the stairs during those treks to classes. Being different seemed to get more pronounced the higher in grade I went.

Almost Not Graduating from High School
Because I Failed Physical Education

Some days after school, and on weekends, holidays, and summer vacations, I worked at the stable, earning riding time. The one big change in my life was that, in my last year in high school, I suddenly wanted to learn everything. I studied hard and got straight As all my senior year. Except for one class—physical education.

That year my riding was peaking with jumping. I was showing a number of horses in the big jumping classes, jumping the fences up to six feet high with five foot spreads. As usual, physical education in school had absolutely no interest to me, and I wasn't any good at anything. I was always the last one picked for teams, and I was generally the laughingstock during the classes. But on a hot-blooded jumper, there was no stopping me. As a matter of fact, the more high-strung the horse was, the better I liked it. I just couldn't catch a ball or toss one through a hoop. Or maybe I simply didn't want to. I'm not quite sure of the answer, but I would guess I really didn't want to do it, because I thought it was a waste of my time.

The gym teacher disliked me from day one. He got very nasty with me many times. He gave me an F for my final grade, which meant I was unable to graduate. He wrote that I was so uncoordinated, I needed remedial classes. My mother went to the school to meet with that teacher and the principal. She brought along a number of photos of me show jumping, including the big ones, 20" x 30", that we'd had matted and framed and hung at home. She let the principal first read the teacher's write-up of how uncoordinated I was and how I needed remedial training. Then she showed him those photos. He didn't say a word. He changed my grade to a C and sent Mom on her way. I was thrilled on graduation day to finally be free.

Graduation Night Disaster

On the night of graduation, my mom and I went to a restaurant to celebrate. I chose a place two towns away to be sure no one from school would see me there, celebrating high-school graduation with my mom. Everyone else, all the normal students and their friends and families, were going to be out on the town partying in big fashion. When we arrived at the restaurant, I requested my usual preference, a corner booth where the lights were dim. Our food had just arrived when I saw people coming toward us. I looked over and saw, to my horror, a big group of students from my graduating class being seated right next to us. Along with them was my twelfth grade English teacher. That was the end of my enjoyable evening. From the moment they spotted me and my mom, they started saying insulting things to me, like that I hadn't gone to the prom, didn't have a date to be with on graduation night, and that I didn't drive. I was in total shock, as was my mom. They were saying these things right in front of my mother and the English teacher. It was one of the most humiliating experiences of my life. I was absolutely dreading having to get up and walk past them to leave.

We didn't even finish our food. Who would? We just asked for the check and got up. We had no choice but to walk past them, and when we did, they all started chanting loudly, including the English teacher himself, "Loser, loser, loser …" Everyone in the whole place was staring at us. By the time we got to the car, I was crying, and so was my mom.

Looking back on that extremely painful memory, I find it beyond belief that an adult with a responsible job like a high school teacher had been the ringleader of those students. He should have been the one to make them stop.

Of course I didn't go to the prom. That was something I only listened to everyone else talking about.

I'm thankful that I developed my intense passion for horses. My teen years were largely consumed by my involvement with riding and showing, which I'll talk about in the next chapter, The Purple and Orange Witch.

Power Point

I strongly encourage parents of AS children and individuals with AS to try very hard to find something you love to do. The teen years are hard enough for even normal, average teens to get through, let alone an AS teen. You need to have an outlet, a special interest, so that you don't focus your energy on the negative aspects of the syndrome.

Chapter 3:

The Purple and Orange Witch: Becoming a Working Student at a Stable to Earn Riding Lessons

When I was about two years old, my mother would take me to a local park to get out of the house and have a diversion. At this park was a pony ride. For twenty-five cents, a child would be led around the track three times on a pony. Thinking it was a good way to entertain me, my mom would bring some change and head over to the pony-ride area.

My first pony ride at age 2

After being led around three times on a little black pony, I simply refused to get off. A lot of quarters were used that day. The girl leading me around and around was probably dizzy by the end of it. That was the beginning of my lifelong passion for horses; my first special interest that truly became all consuming.

I wanted to play with plastic horses instead of Barbie dolls. My mother loves dolls, and when she was a young girl she would sew beautiful outfits for her dolls. She was looking forward to doing the same for my dolls, but there weren't going to be any dolls for me. Not a one. Horses only, and lots of them. I was totally obsessed with horses.

In first grade, I would spend most of my time gazing out the windows, imagining myself galloping across the meadow. One day my teacher asked me what I was looking at so intently out the window. In a matter-of-fact tone I explained, in great detail, that I could see myself galloping through the lush pasture on a white horse, with his mane and tail flowing in the wind. I could feel the warmth of the sun on my skin, and the power of the horse beneath me. After my elaborate description, the teacher just stared at me. The next day my mother was called to school.

Mucking Stalls

One really bad thing about horses is that it costs a lot of money to be involved in the sport. I guess that's why Thoroughbred racing, and sometimes polo, is often referred to as the Sport of Kings. My mom had no money for me to do something like this. One Sunday afternoon in early spring, when I was about eleven or twelve, we were driving along a main thoroughfare, when I spotted a huge horse show going on. I demanded the car be stopped so I could go see this event. I literally dragged my mother over to an arena where jumping was going on. I'd seen it in books, but never in person. One after another, riders would enter the arena and jump the sixteen obstacles in a specific pattern. Scoring was based on clean jumps and the time it took to get around the course. The jumps were six feet high, and some had a spread of four or five feet. Right then, I announced to my mother that

I was going to do that someday. Normally my mom is behind me 100 percent, but being the realistic person she is, she told me that this was a rich man's sport and cost lots of money. I wasn't going to accept that. I wanted to do this, and that's all there was to it. I would find a way, and over the next seven years, I did. Eventually, I was the one jumping over six-foot high fences and winning state championships. It was a long, hard road getting there. I now realize that if I didn't have Asperger's syndrome, I never would have pulled it off. It was my laser focus and unrelenting drive that made it possible.

There was a big riding stable about half an hour away from my home. I learned that they had a working student program there, which meant that if you did a certain amount of work, you earned a lesson or riding time. It was a huge facility. The main level consisted of big 12' x 12' stalls where privately owned horses were housed; the lounge and office; and the indoor arena, which was about 60' x 150'. Downstairs were all the school horses, and the big tack room that contained saddles and bridles for each of those horses. There was a huge outdoor arena as well, with bleachers on both sides of it. The stable was my sanctuary for most of my youth, and it shaped my character and my drive to achieve goals. It was the best prescription for the Asperger's syndrome I didn't know I had.

I was about twelve when I started working there. There were several other kids my age, maybe a few older than myself. We all had one goal—we desperately wanted to ride horses. They'd start us mucking out stalls, a seemingly endless number of stalls. It was hard work, but I thrived on it. Any minute near a horse was a great minute. As I was cleaning a stall and filling my wheelbarrow, I'd study the horse in that particular stall. I'd watch every move it made, and would analyze why it was doing a particular thing. The horses were just as fascinated with me. Often they would come near me as I worked, and gently touch their faces against mine, or make some other gesture that indicated they liked me. I felt quite smug about this, because the horses never paid attention to the other kids when they were cleaning the stalls. I had a special kinship with the horses, both in the stables and, as I'd eventually discover, when I was on their backs.

My drive to ride and to one day be great at it far surpassed that of any of the other working students. I worked twice as hard and twice as long as they, and thus got twice as many lessons and riding time. I hope I'm not going to offend anyone with this, but there was a worker at the stable, an older guy name Jesse. One day, as I was scurrying about working, he leaned on his pitchfork and said, "You never stop moving. Creepin' Jesus. Yup, that's what you are, Creepin' Jesus." From then on, that's what he called me.

I was a natural-born rider. Eventually I began to ride the more advanced horses, and then the elite horses that were owned by the stable. When I reached that point, the people who boarded their horses at the stable asked me to ride their horses in the jumper divisions at the shows. I was in heaven. There were days when I could barely ride all the horses I had to ride. What a wonderful problem to have.

Getting to that point was an extremely long hard road. After doing my stint mucking out stalls, I was assigned to everything else that needed to be done there, like picking rocks out of the paddocks. I would go into the big paddock where the privately owned horses got their turn-out time, taking along a shovel, pick, and gloves. We had to remove the rocks so the horses wouldn't injure their hooves by stepping on them. There were lots of little rocks, but also plenty of big ones that I had to dig out, lift into the wheelbarrow, and then go dump the heavy load. And then do it again. It was especially unpleasant when it was ninety-eight degrees out in the blistering sun.

Painting endless fences was another task. Not only the pristine white post-and-rail fencing around the entire facility, but the jumps that we used. Especially before shows, everything had to be painted.

The best job was when they assigned me to run the school horse barn. In hindsight, I really think I assigned myself to that. In any case, I was responsible for the feeding, watering, and care of about twenty-six horses; cleaning all the saddles and bridles daily; plus getting each horse ready for the lessons that went on all day long. I used to boss around the other working students, delegating work to them as well. There was a tremendous amount of work to be done. This was how I spent my summers throughout junior high and high school. I loved every minute of it.

Defying the Riding Instructor Who Demanded I Get Back on a Crazy Horse

One of my very first clashes with someone in authority was when I was fourteen. I was in a group lesson in the outdoor arena with about twelve other students, on a hot summer morning. I was riding a horse named Lollipop, whom I hated and was a bit scared of. Nothing much scared me concerning horses, but this one did. I never trusted any horse that constantly showed the whites of its eyes. Our instructor, Ralph, asked everyone to pick up a canter. I gave Lollipop the signal to canter, and she took off at a full gallop. There was no stopping her. I watched the ground whiz by as I did everything I could to bring her under control. I tried to pull her into smaller and smaller circles. By this time everyone else had stopped. Most of the students had got off their horses. (It is safest to get off your horse when another one is out of control, in case your horse decides to join the wild one.) Finally, after what seemed an eternity, I got that miserable horse to stop. She was still dancing around in a tiny circle, but was under control. Right then, I jumped off her back. Ralph ordered me to get back on her. There was no way I'd ever get on her back, not then, not ever. I refused and started leading Lollipop out of the arena, taking her back to the barn. Ralph yelled at me to get back there, but I kept going. I put the horse away and then went upstairs to the lounge, to sit down and calm my nerves.

I stayed in the lounge until it was time for my mom to pick me up. She arrived early and came looking for me. Apparently she'd run into Ralph. He lit into her, saying that she needed to do something about her daughter, who displayed defiant behavior to authority. She had no idea what he was talking about. I filled her in when I saw her. She was quite mad, because it was really a safety issue. She didn't want me back on that miserable Lollipop either. Ralph didn't speak to me for the next two years. In hindsight, I can see it was ridiculous for him to act like that with a teenager.

Strangely, years later when he was talking to me again, he asked me one day to ride home with him in his new car. He had forgotten his saddle, and all trainers used their own saddles. I went with him. It was only about a ten-minute drive. Once at his apartment, he grabbed me and started passionately kissing me. French kissing, to be exact. That was my first experience kissing like that. It was quite shocking, but fun. We kissed for quite some time. He didn't try anything else, just the kissing. I was sixteen then.

Reaching My Dream of Jumping High Fences

My jumping days were finally a reality. The fences were getting higher and higher, and wider and wider. Two of the instructors at the stable, Mary and Shirley, had us do exercises designed to improve balance and confidence while jumping. We would tie up the reins and not use them, just ride the horse by using our legs and body weight. In addition, when we approached the jumps, we held our arms out like wings. Eventually we'd hold our hands on the tops of our heads. Try jumping a full course of sixteen obstacles that are 4' 6" in height with 4' spreads, including a triple combination on the last three fences, with no reins and your hands on top of your head. Once we mastered that, we removed our stirrups as well. They made a real rider out of me.

Reaching my dream of jumping big fences. I was seventeen here.

The more difficult the horse, the more I liked them. As I came to learn, the more talented horses are the more challenging to deal with. They would have lots of quirks, and you'd have to figure out how to deal with them in order to ride the horses to their fullest capability. That was my forte, because I had that special rapport that no one else seemed to have. I could take a common school horse and make it look like a $50,000 horse. This bugged a lot of people, and most of all it bugged the Purple and Orange Witch.

Jumping at the big Junior Essex Troop show

She was the manager of the stable. She earned the name the Purple and Orange Witch because she always wore cheap-looking purple polyester pants and an equally cheap-looking orange blouse. Plus, she acted like a witch. I was directly to the point even then.

Junior Essex Troop Horse Show

Each year was the annual horse show at Junior Essex Troop in West Orange, New Jersey. It was awesome. Riding in that show was one of my dreams. In addition to showing in the jumper classes on several horses, I became quite the entrepreneur, braiding manes and tails. I had become an expert at braiding horses' manes and tails for shows, and would get the word out between rides that I was available. In no time flat I'd be booked, with people clamoring for my services. Manes are easy to do, but tails are intricate, and not everyone can do them. I watched the pros do it and studied the process, and then practiced until I got good at it. I'd make hundreds of dollars within a few hours. The money would go toward something horse-related, of course.

One show I'll never forget was when I was riding a horse named Everest. I was awaiting my turn to go into the arena and jump my round. The sky was getting darker and darker by the second. Thunder rumbled in the distance. They were contemplating waiting for the storm to pass, but then my number was called and I entered the arena. It started pouring like mad. I picked up a canter and proceeded to the first jump. Just as Everest was lifting us over the obstacle, a bolt of lightning struck close by; the thunder crashed immediately overhead. I was blinded by both the flash and the torrential downpour. Someone took a photo at that exact moment. It looked like Everest and I were struck by lightning, because the streak was directly past us. As soon as we landed, I rapidly exited the arena to safety.

Learning How Spiteful Jealous People Can Be

Something else I learned during my teen years at the stable was just how mean someone can be when they are jealous of you, for whatever reason. Everyone at the stable was always nice to me, and some went out of their way to help me out if they could. Everyone, that is, except the Purple and Orange Witch. From here on I'll refer to her as the P&OW.

The P&OW's two daughters, Shelly and Terry, each had a very expensive horse. Trainers were always working with them, and they went to every show around to try to win ribbons. P&OW stopped at nothing to pursue this for Shelly and Terry. She would regularly have horse shows right at the stable, big shows, with lots of people from surrounding areas bringing their horses to compete. Her daughters did very well at these shows. What a surprise that was, considering she was the one paying the judges.

Then along comes this poor kid who works for her rides, and she rides school horses in the jumpers and docs better than the P&OW's two daughters. As I learned from my instructors and others there, the P&OW went ballistic when I started competing in the jumping classes her daughters were in. In equitation classes and pleasure classes, the judging is based on subjective factors. In jumpers, it's cut and dried. Either you jump a fence cleanly, or a rail comes down, or the horse refuses a jump, or the horse and/or rider falls. And then there is the time it takes to complete the course. There are no subjective factors at all in jumping. That suited me just fine. Those were the classes I'd beat her daughters in. In a big way.

After winning an open jumper division on a horse owned by the stable, the P&OW saw to it that I wasn't allowed to ride that horse anymore. My instructors were angry, too, but their hands were tied. Everyone knew she was jealous that I could ride better than her daughters, even though I was riding lesser caliber horses than her daughters.

The P&OW did all sorts of things to me because of this. One of my instructors, Rick, had bought a spectacular horse that he imported from Germany. I was totally enthralled by the horse, and everyone knew it, because I talked about it enough. One day I watched Rick riding the horse, and when he was done, he asked me to get on and cool the horse out for him. I was beside myself with joy. I was in the saddle faster than you could blink an eye. I felt like I was sitting on top of the world. Others who were riding in the arena at the time were cheering for me, because they knew I was so thrilled. Right then I saw the P&OW heading down the small hill with her fists clenched. She called Rick over to the fence, and I saw her mouth going a hundred miles an hour to him, obviously in a rage. She turned and stormed away, back to the office. Rick walked slowly toward me and said he felt bad, but he had to ask me to get off the horse. The P&OW was furious that I was on its back. He said how ugly it was, and he was embarrassed, but she was his boss. How pathetic was it that a grown woman was so enraged that a seventeen-year-old kid was sitting on some horse to cool it out? But she knew how happy it made me, and she got her happiness out of taking mine away.

Then there was the horse she purchased for Shelly, a jumper from Holland that cost some outrageous sum of money. The horse was huge, and Shelly was terrified of it. She rode the mare maybe three times, and fell off it each time. That was it. From then on, that huge animal stayed locked in her stall twenty-four hours a day. They never even put it out in the paddock, so it could move around and see sunlight. I thought that was extremely mean, not to mention a waste of a talented horse. Knowing what the answer would be, I still asked my instructors if there was any I could ride that horse. Both of them replied the same: that the P&OW would never allow me to ride the horse her daughter was terrified of, and worst of all, that I'd do great on. Everyone knew she was jealous of me. So, that horse just continued to stand in its stall. It eventually took up weaving, which is when a bored horse stands in one place and weaves its head and shoulders from right to left endlessly, for hours at a time.

The Purple & Orange Witch did lots of little things to me over the years, but it was just another lesson in life. In hindsight, I wonder if my Asperger's syndrome played a factor in her feelings toward me. I think, though, it was simply that she was jealous that I rode better than her two daughters.

Wanting to Spend Every Possible Moment by a Horse

An elderly man worked on the main level of the barn, where all the privately owned horses were stabled. He had about twenty-five horses in his charge. He'd like to leave early on Sundays, around 2 p.m., instead of staying until 5, but he was worried the horses would run out of water to drink if he left that early and didn't top off their buckets. He asked me if, for $1.00—yes, one dollar—before I left at 6 on Sundays, I'd go around with the hose and fill each horse's water bucket. I happily accepted my new position as water girl. It gave me yet another opportunity to be with each horse, to have my special communication time with them. I did that job for years. In the winter, though, my hands would literally be frozen by the time I was done, the skin cracking open from the cold. It didn't faze me a bit. I still loved every minute of it.

Chapter 4:

College Years: My New Ticket to Freedom

Entering college was like a ticket to freedom. The cliques were gone, the bullies were nowhere to be found. It seemed that everyone was off doing their own thing and couldn't be bothered by any of the above. I enjoyed this tremendously.

During my final year of high school, I couldn't decide what I wanted to do with my life. I gravitated to psychology, and had applied to Montclair State College in Montclair, New Jersey, to major in this field. I think in some corner of my mind, I wanted to go into psychology to perhaps find answers about myself, to discover why I was so different. So different, in fact, that I mostly felt like I was from another planet and had been transported here by accident. On the inside, I wanted to make friends, but on the outside this wasn't apparent to anyone. I was hoping, praying, that inside one of those psychology textbooks would be the answer to this mystery. Little did I know that there was an answer, discovered by Dr. Hans Asperger, only it was still in Austria. It had not yet reached this side of the pond, and wouldn't until 1994. I started college in 1977.

The campus was beautiful, set among sprawling hills. The first few weeks were stressful, as I had to locate the buildings my classes were in and get used to a whole new system and way of life. Of course, no one made any attempt to be friends with me, but that was nothing new. When I tried to initiate conversation with someone, I could see their uneasy response. I heard about the campus pub, located downstairs in the student union building. I went there, by myself, naturally, and felt extremely out of place and uncomfortable. I would order a soda and sit by the bar, being the socially inept person that I was, especially back then. I felt like I was invisible, because all around me were lively conversations, people mingling, having fun. And there I'd sit, all alone, not quite sure why I was staying there, but I would. I guess I kept hoping that one day I'd be a part of the fun. It never happened.

One of the reasons I continued going to the pub was to see Larry Logic. That was my nickname for him. He was my professor for logic, and his first name was Larry. I thought he was mighty cute, and he was really smart. Brainy guys are my thing. Larry appeared to be a loner, as I never saw him talking to anyone outside of class, not even other professors. He frequented the pub, where he'd buy one beer and sit in a corner and read a book or newspaper. That was his ritual. I'd just sit there, too, and wish either he'd come over by me, or that I'd get the courage to go over by him. Neither happened. During the next semester I learned the shocking news. One night on the local news Larry Logic's picture was on the screen, and the reporter said he'd been found dead from a self-inflicted gunshot wound. I was devastated for months. I sought out professors from his department to try to find out anything they might know. They were not talking. It was actually my English professor who filled me in on some details. Apparently Larry Logic suffered from depression, which stemmed from not being able to make friends or get a girlfriend. In hindsight, I think he was an Aspie. That was a real shame. A bright guy like that killed himself.

Earning Membership into the National Honor Society in Psychology

I loved reading about psychology, and it came very easy to me. I was getting As on all my tests. During my second year I was notified that I had been selected to be a member of Psi Chi, the National Honor Society in Psychology. I was very surprised and excited. They had a lovely ceremony for the new members, with a reception afterward. My mom was there, and it was an enjoyable evening. That was my last year at Montclair State College. I had applied to Bloomfield College, and was accepted into their nursing program.

Volunteering at a Local Hospital

During my time at Montclair State College, I decided to do some volunteer work at a hospital near my home. It just seemed like a nice thing to do. I did that each Saturday morning from 8 a.m. until 1 p.m., for two years. They assigned me to a surgery floor, where patients who had things like hip replacements, knee replacements, pelvic fractures, and things like that recovered from their surgery. The staff on that floor was less than thrilled at my presence, and made it quite obvious that I didn't fit in and didn't belong. The nurses ignored me, and a few were downright nasty to me. I was used to this sort of behavior by this time, and it didn't faze me. I had found something much more rewarding to do there than help out the nurses.

The majority of the patients were elderly, and were hospitalized for long periods of time. Often they had no family or friends to come visit them. I would sit with each one of them to talk to them—or rather, mostly listen to them—and they were comforted at having a friend. This became my ritual. I kept in touch with many of them long after they were discharged. It was a rewarding experience, and it was during this time that I decided to become a nurse.

As I mentioned earlier, I almost didn't get into the nursing program, because I did badly on the reading section of their entrance exam. The director of the nursing program, Dr. Fran McLaughlin, wanted to meet me in person. She told me about my score on the reading exam, and that the program requires a great deal of reading. After talking to me, though, she stated that she felt I was worth the risk. She wanted to give me a chance, so I was accepted into the program. If she hadn't give me that chance, who knows where I'd be today. I've been thankful to her ever since.

When I took tests, different things annoyed me. For reading, I'd have to read some lengthy, extremely boring piece, and then answer questions about it. I simply couldn't get myself to read it. This is an Asperger's thing. Once I got that in my head, that was it. No one was going to make me read it. Obviously, I'd get all the answers incorrect for that section. It was different in classes, because I *wanted* to learn the material. Then there was no stopping me, another Asperger's trait!

My Lack of Social Skills Becomes Obvious

My serious lack of social skills would eventually become obvious, but the first two years at Bloomfield College went quite smoothly. I was thriving in the classes, and the people were nice. My favorite professor was Dr. Russo, and he taught the full year of anatomy and physiology. He had a great personality for teaching, and made the class fun and interesting. During the end of the first semester of his class, I broke my arm during an ice-dancing practice.

Me and my ice dancing partner during a practice session

I had been ice dancing for several years, and loved it. My ice-dancing partner, Richard, and I were rehearsing for an ice show. Richard had seen some really slick footwork on TV that one of the Olympic skaters had been doing. So of course we attempted this feat. We had actually mastered it, only now we were trying to do it at a faster pace. I was facing backward when we fell, and I remember putting out my left arm to break the fall. I actually heard and felt the bone snap when I hit the ice. Having a very high pain tolerance, I calmly got up off the ice and skated to the exit door, and then walked into the office to ask the secretary to call me an ambulance.

"Why do you need an ambulance?" she asked.

I lifted up my left arm, with my right hand supporting the break, which was just beyond my wrist. I let go with my right hand, and the fractured area flopped down. The secretary nearly fainted. I thought that was pretty funny.

Age nineteen, ice dancing.

Finally I was at the hospital in the emergency room. After my arm was X-rayed, the orthopedic surgeon on call came in to set my arm and put a cast on it. Since he was going to have to do some tugging and manipulation to line up the fractures, they called in the anesthesiologist to give me a bit of sedation. I was actually having fun at this little "party," and considered the broken arm a minor annoyance. In conversation, I mentioned that I was a student, and final exams were in two days. The anesthesiologist asked me what I was studying, and I told him I was going for my bachelor of science in nursing. He asked, "Why don't you go on to be a CRNA, a certified registered nurse anesthetist?"

I had no idea what that was, so he explained. He told me that Columbia University had the highest rated program in the country, and I would first need to have two years of, basically, premed courses. A full year of general chemistry, followed the next year by a full year of organic chemistry, a full year of physics, etc.

During my second year at Bloomfield College, I was on the work study program. I was a graphic arts designer, with an official office right next to the president of the college. I did the layout and design of all of the college's publications and flyers, and the monthly newsletter. I had a great time doing it, and there was always some crazy thing going on. I got to know all of the administrators well, and they seemed to like me. I looked forward to my twenty hours there each week.

I'm sure that during my last two years at Bloomfield College, my lack of social functioning became obvious to everyone—my professors, classmates, and the patients themselves. Of course, I had difficulty interacting with everyone, and they probably spent a lot of time talking about the "oddball." The other students all formed study groups, but I was on my own. I couldn't figure out why that was.

I did well on tests, but I guess my interactions with patients when we did our clinical training was rather unusual. I would talk to them as little as possible, and only perform the necessary activity, such as administer medications, give an injection, take blood pressure. You get the picture. I'd never just stand there and chat with a patient, as my classmates did.

One day, about a month before graduation, I was doing my clinical training, and checked in on a young female patient. She was in a lot of emotional distress about her condition and her family. I sat down on the end of her bed and got her talking about her problems, and once she talked about it all, she felt much better. She apparently mentioned this to my instructor, Carolyn. Several days later, Carolyn asked to see me in her office. *Now what?* I thought.

She began by saying, "That young lady that you talked at length to the other day told me how good you made her feel. I have a very faint glimmer of hope that you're starting to see the whole picture." She proceeded to tell me that all the other nursing professors were troubled by my lack of social interacting with others, especially patients. "We don't know if you can see the whole picture, if you are putting together all the pieces of the puzzle."

Yesterday, which was February 22, 2011, twenty-eight years later, that conversation flashed into my mind. I stopped over at Dr. Lee Day's office to pick up information on CARD services to include in my book. She mentioned that one of the difficulties that people with Asperger's syndrome have is not being able to see the whole picture. Instead, they focus on the individual components. I started to cry, remembering that conversation with Carolyn. And I then became embarrassed, realizing just how bizarre I must have seemed to all those professors, students, and patients. How much grief I must have caused them. Dr. Day handed me a tissue and suggested I forget it. I had no control over how my brain worked, and should just let it go.

I know she's right, but I still feel embarrassed. The only good part is that once I was out of college and actually working, I saw the whole picture very well, and turned out to be a first-rate anesthetist.

Fooled by Someone in Authority

I will never forget the Good Reverend, as I'll call him. This particular reverend had a church just down the street from the campus. In fact, the nurses' pinning ceremony was held there each year for graduation, and he would preside. He spent a lot of time on the campus taking photos of activities and giving the photos to the people for free. That was his hobby. It turned out to be quite the interesting pastime.

One day he was at the student center giving someone the photos he had taken of them, really great portraits in black and white. I thought that my mom would love photos of me like that, so I asked him about getting some done. He happily agreed, and we set up an appointment for me to go to his home, which was right next to the church, as that was where his studio was. So, several days later I showed up for the photo shoot. He greeted me at the door and escorted me down into his basement. As I walked down the stairs, I could see camera equipment all over, like tripods, umbrella lights, you name it. Quite a setup. Once down there, he wanted to show me his work, and headed into a small, rather dimly lit room. There, plastered on all the walls, were photos, most of them of topless or totally nude girls. As I looked around, I realized I knew many of the girls, fellow students. First I was shocked at the girls I recognized, because never, in a million years, would I have thought they'd participate in something like that. Then, most obviously, I was quite freaked out that the Good Reverend was into all this. Back in those days, I wasn't so jaded, like I am now. Now when I see stuff like this on TV, I'm not surprised in the least.

Of course I wanted to run out of there, but my mind was racing about what to do. Reluctantly, I decided to stay. We then went back into the studio area, and he had me sit on a chair in front of the camera. He took an endless amount of portrait shots, many different angles of my face. He then suggested I get some sexy photos while I was there, and that I should go ahead and take my top off. He made a reference to the photos in the other room, and how happy the girls had been once they had the photos to give their boyfriends. I declined his offer.

He walked over to a tall metal cabinet I hadn't noticed earlier, and unlocked the chains that were around the handles. A lump formed in my throat. Opening the doors, he told me to come over and select something to change into from his selection. Looking in the cabinet, I saw all kinds of sex outfits, as I'll call them—lace corsets, leather wear, S&M props, and stuff I'll leave to your imagination. He was looking at me rather oddly by now, and I realized his breathing was audible. *Exit time*, I thought, and with that I rapidly walked past him, ran up the stairs, and out the door to the freedom of outside. I was shaking at that point. I walked home really fast and told my mother about the whole incident.

The next day when I went to classes, I saw one of the girls, whose topless photo I had seen the day before on the Good Reverend's wall. I asked to talk to her in private. We went outside and sat under a big tree. I told her what had happened to me at his house, and that I saw the photos of her on the wall. She burst out crying, and told me of how he had tricked her into letting him take those photos. She'd never had intentions like that to begin with, and had just wanted the same sort of photos as I had, some black and white portraits for her family. She said that after he'd taken the portrait shots, he'd told her to take her top off. She politely declined, but he kept pressuring her, saying it was okay because he was a reverend and he wasn't going to tell anyone. He kept repeating how much her boyfriend would enjoy such photos, continuing to pressure her, until she took her clothing off to pose topless for him. She was horrified to learn he had those pictures up on his wall. Apparently, he hadn't taken her into that little room.

Later that afternoon, I saw the Good Reverend. He came over to me to give me a big brown envelope with my photos in it. He seemed extremely nervous. I didn't say anything to him, except to thank him for the photos. That night I told my mother about my talk with the student who had given in to his pressure. The next day my mom called the president of the college, whom she had met on many occasions. She told him the whole story of the Good Reverend, of what had happened to me, the girl I had spoken to, and that there were quite a number of other students whose photos I had seen, including the provocative nude ones. No one ever saw the Good Reverend after that. I guess he got sent somewhere else. I would have loved to be a fly on the wall when the president called him in to chat.

Selected for Who's Who Among Students in American Universities & Colleges

The four years at Bloomfield College were very productive ones. I spent a lot of time studying. One peculiar thing I always did was study in the college library, because it was so silent; and I'd seek out the farthest, most dimly lit cubicle I could find. Other people noticed this, and often asked me why I had to go there. I never had a real answer, other than I felt comfortable in that atmosphere. Today I'd be able to answer that I have Asperger's syndrome, that's why.

At the beginning of my second year there, I decided to join the yearbook committee. I figured that with my graphic arts experience, it would be a good opportunity, and maybe I'd make friends with someone. By the third meeting of the committee, no one showed up. All those years, from 1980 until 2011, I thought people just were not interested. Last night I got on a laughing jag, when I suddenly realized that all those people dropped off the committee because I was there. I'd always had a talent for clearing out a room, and obviously that's what happened. They didn't want to be with the space alien, which is how I've often felt.

I couldn't stand the idea of the college not having a yearbook, so I became the entire yearbook committee. For the ensuing year, at any given time my dining room table was covered from one end to another with everything it takes to make a yearbook. With the exception of the senior portraits, I did all the photography of everything, like student clubs, campus activities, the campus itself. I did the entire layout, design, typing, even the cover of the yearbook, which I designed as something unique. At the end of the year, in my hand was the final edition of the college yearbook.

For my efforts to produce a yearbook all by myself, and for the other volunteer things I did on campus, I was selected for two consecutive years into Who's Who Among Students in American Universities & Colleges. It was quite prestigious, and I was very proud of my accomplishments. I didn't know at the time that my Asperger's laser focus got me through it all.

Discovering I Have Visual Thinking

Graduation from Bloomfield College was behind me. I was working part-time as a nurse in an ER while attending Montclair State College, taking those two years of premed classes so I could apply to Columbia University for their CRNA program.

The first years of general chemistry and physics were beyond a nightmare for me. I am convinced that the part of the brain that is designated for mathematics had been totally devoid since birth. Even in high school I barely made it through my math classes. Even to this day, just the sight of numbers makes me anxious and sick to my stomach. Somehow I made it through that year.

I was terrified, however, of the coming year of organic chemistry. I had heard story after story from other students about how complex it was, and many people flunked it. I was really getting scared. For some reason, I always sat in the front row in all my classes, right in front of the professor. So, on that first day in September of 1984, I sat right there in front of Dr. John Isadore. To the students, he was known simply as Izzy. Little did I know, but on that day I was about to make an unusual discovery about myself. Izzy used that first day to tell us what he expected of everyone, and then pretty much said go have a nice day, buy the book, and see you tomorrow. I went to the bookstore and bought the creepy-looking book, which was literally four inches thick. I was too unnerved even to open the book. But that night I managed to read the first chapter.

The next day in class, Izzy started talking about organic chemistry. As he drew chemical structures on the blackboard, he started explaining the basics, saying our knowledge needed to grow from the basics, like building blocks. The more he talked and drew, the more fascinated I became. Understanding organic chemistry involves being able to imagine the chemical structure in your mind and going from there. I was able to see in my mind, like it was a huge movie screen, all these chemical structures, and I could mentally manipulate them into whatever shape was necessary. Organic chemistry rapidly grew to be my favorite course of any I ever took. I was getting 100s on every test, and having a blast learning everything. I felt quite smug that this was so easy for me, and I would always shoot my hand up to answer Izzy's questions. Eventually he asked me to not raise my hand, because he knew I knew it all, and he wanted others to answer the questions. I simply could not understand why others found this subject so difficult. People were flunking out left and right. Of course, now I realize why it was so easy for me. AS brains are great at visual thinking. Izzy was a terrific teacher too, and I still remember him well.

Starting at Columbia University in New York City

Who would ever think that someone whose grandfather was a coal miner in Wilkes-Barre, Pennsylvania, and had grown up in a house that used a wringer washer, would one day attend an Ivy League school like Columbia. I was really scared to make this next move, because I was used to the comforts of my little house in the little town. Now I was going to be living on the twelfth floor of a high-rise on the upper west side of Manhattan, right by Columbia-Presbyterian Medical Center and the George Washington Bridge. The building was on Haven Avenue.

I can still remember the day my mom helped me move into the apartment, with its window that overlooked a huge park. We quickly learned that this area was called Washington Heights, the biggest crack capitol of the United States. You could watch tons of drug transactions going on, any time of day or night, punctuated by an occasional gunshot. It helped keep the trauma center at the hospital hopping. So here I was, an Aspie, in the middle of a war zone. My stress level maxed out on a daily basis.

Our classes for the first year were held in the medical library, which was in the main building of the medical school for Columbia University. That's where I also learned about New York City cockroaches. My class for the nurse anesthesia program had only six students in it, besides myself. We met one day to go study in the library. When we got there, all the meeting rooms were filled. The librarian told us to go downstairs to the lower levels, because those rooms might be unoccupied. We ended up five levels down. It was cold out, so everyone had worn a coat. They were hanging on the backs of our chairs. Something caught my eye, and I turned and looked down. At first I didn't realize what I was seeing. It was like an ocean of giant cockroaches—or palmetto bugs, as we learned—and they were crawling all over the place. I started screaming and jumped on top of the table, pointing on the floor. Within seconds the rest of them were up there with me, screaming. One of the other students got the courage to jump down and run out, and everyone followed suit. As we ran, we could hear the crunching sounds of the bugs being stepped on. Those horrible bugs would become a regular sight for me while I lived in Manhattan. No matter how much roach stuff you'd put around, there would be one waiting for you when you opened a cabinet, pulled out some clothing, just anywhere. Another stressor.

One day the professor announced that our classes were going to start meeting downtown at Roosevelt Hospital, which was near Rockefeller Center and Lincoln Center. As a matter of fact, he wanted us to catch a bus or subway down there that day to get familiarized with the faculty and the facility. Panic rose in me. One of my classmates decided to ride the bus, the M5. Everyone else took the subway. I went with the bus ride. Just the thought of the subway gave me chills.

We caught the bus on the corner of West 168th Street and Broadway. The ride down to West 59th Street was very educational. Sort of like going around the world. We passed a multitude of ethnic areas, each one very distinct. We also passed an area on the Upper West Side where lots of multimillionaires lived, and a number of old cathedrals with beautiful architecture.

Suddenly Annie said, "Here's our stop!" As she jumped up to get off the bus, I rapidly followed her as if I was attached to her. We no sooner stepped off the bus than it pulled away, making a loud hissing sound just before it lurched forward. Hundreds of people were walking all over everywhere, seemingly coming out of the woodwork. Sort of like those palmetto bugs. I can vividly remember looking up and seeing that I was totally surrounded by skyscrapers. I froze. My Asperger senses were maxed out. The sounds of all the bumper-to-bumper traffic, with yellow cabs making up at least one third of the cars, people talking, buses idling, men on scaffolding above us using drills; the overwhelming smell of car fumes, hot dogs from a street vendor, and the stench from a nearby subway stairwell flooded my head. I couldn't move or speak. I could just about breathe. I slowly started turning to look all around me. Annie was no longer in sight. A feeling of panic set in. Now what? I had no idea which way to go. Suddenly I heard her yelling my name, and turned to look for her. I was very thankful to see her. We walked to Roosevelt Hospital, a few blocks from where I was standing. I was totally exhausted by this point, and couldn't believe I would have to do that all over again to get back home.

As luck would have it, one of the senior students offered to let me take over the lease on her apartment as soon as she graduated. The apartment was directly across the street from Roosevelt Hospital, on West 59th Street, overlooking the Hudson River. The unit was on the thirty-first floor. I'm terrified of heights, and when I first went in to see the apartment, I was too scared to go by the window. The view of the New Jersey skyline was truly spectacular at night, shimmering on the river.

The building had quite the fancy lobby, complete with a doorman, who quickly learned everyone's names and unit number. I was never at ease living on the thirty-first floor, least of all when something strange started happening. One morning, Mom and I walked out of our apartment, heading for to the elevator. Written on the walls was the word PYRO, and cigarette butts and matches were all over the place. I didn't sleep for days after that, and each day the word PYRO was written in more places. Everyone was getting nervous. One morning just after Christmas, at about five thirty, the fire alarms went off. My mom and I, along with everyone else, started running down thirty-one flights of stairs. By the time we got to the bottom, our legs were like jelly. We could hardly stand up. It turned out that someone had thrown a lit cigarette down the trash chute. Someone else had stuffed their Christmas tree down the chute, and the tree had caught fire. The fire was actually contained inside the metal trash chute, but it made lots of smoke. This was just what an Aspie needed for stress.

Another test of my Asperger nerves was on my birthday, when I got stuck in the elevator between the thirty-first and thirtieth floors for nearly two hours. My mom's friends, two British sisters with heavy but elegant British accents, had come to spend the day with us to celebrate my birthday. It was July 9, 1987, and I had made reservations at the Plaza Hotel's Palm Court for afternoon tea. My mom and I went there about once a month, on Friday afternoons after I got out of classes and the operating room. On this particular day, Sofia and Diana would be joining us.

Back in the day, I was quite slim and fashionable. I was wearing a short petal pink dress, with white buttons down the front. It wasn't exceptionally low cut, but enough to highlight my chest. I had on a big white picture hat and white high heels. Sofia and Diana had come up to our apartment, and now we were all making our way to the elevator. We had just stepped out of the elevator into the lobby, when Diana realized she'd forgotten her purse. Sofia and my mom sat on a couch to wait while Diana and I went back up to the apartment. After getting her purse, we returned to the elevator. A very creepy, sleazy-looking man was standing there. He kept looking me up and down, making me very uneasy. I wasn't looking forward to riding down to the main floor with him in the elevator with us. My instinct was to skip the ride and wait for the next one, but Diana thought that was silly.

Against my inner feeling, we got into the elevator with the creep. The doors had no sooner shut, than the elevator lurched and slammed to a stop. The doors opened, and my heart dropped to my toes. There we were, stuck between the thirty-first and thirtieth floor. You could see down the shaft in the gap between it and the doors. Diana thought this was hilarious. I was ready to faint. Just thinking of it now makes me nervous. The creep made some comment about how great this was, because now he could look at me longer. The panic I felt inside was mounting by the second. Though I tried to maintain my composure, sweat poured down my spine, and my throat was as dry as sandpaper. Back then there were no cell phones. I pounded on the wall of the elevator, yelling for help. What a great way to spend my birthday.

Forty-five minutes into this nightmare, I heard voices yelling, and it sounded like they were close by. Sure enough, it was the elevator servicemen. They called up to us that they were working on the problem and to just sit tight. Easy for them to say. It made me feel a bit better, but not much. Every now and then the elevator would lurch, or drop ten or twenty feet. With each drop the elevator doors would open, and we would be between floors. All I kept picturing was the car suddenly dropping all the way to the bottom, and what the impact was going to be like. Diana's mouth never stopped this whole entire time. She continued to think this whole situation was a blast. She kept telling stories, chatting with the creepy guy, trying to talk to me. I ignored her, working hard at tuning her out, since my brain was beyond being overloaded.

An hour and a half later, the elevator began to descend in a normal fashion. When it arrived at the bottom and the doors opened, I was ready to cry. My mother was as pale as a ghost. I was in no mood to go to the Plaza, or anywhere for that matter. All

I wanted to do was go sit somewhere by myself, in peace and quiet. Sofia and Diana would not have it, and insisted we continue with our plans. I was madder than a hornet, and made my feelings obvious. My mom wasn't much better. She had been worried to pieces all during the elevator escapade, not knowing what was going to happen. I was glad when we were done with the afternoon tea. When we got back to the apartment, I lay down on the couch and slept for several hours. From that day forward, I was terrified to get into that elevator.

Anyone Can Fit in New York City

One nice thing about New York City, a person never has to worry about fitting in. It's like the melting pot of the world, and anything goes. What a relief that was. Also, once we learned our way around the city, there was no stopping us from hopping buses to go somewhere new. From the Cloisters Museum on the northern edge of the city, to South Street Seaport down by the World Trade Center, Mom and I did up the town.

Christmas in New York is unsurpassed. There is nothing like walking down Fifth Avenue with all its world-famous window displays, such as at Sak's, and arriving at the Channel Gardens, which lead to 30 Rockefeller Plaza and that magnificent Christmas tree. Even though I hadn't ice skated in several years, not since breaking my arm, I couldn't resist skating on the ice arena there, right in front of that towering tree and amid all the grandeur of Rockefeller Plaza. I felt mighty happy to be out there on that famous ice. One night we stayed at the plaza until 11 p.m. Since it was just before Christmas, even at that hour the sidewalks were packed with people. It was lightly snowing. My mom and I decided to walk back to our apartment. Singing Christmas carols at the top of our lungs seemed like a fun idea, which we did all the way up to Central Park West. Not one person gave us a second glance. That's what I loved about NYC.

Another highlight was living near Lincoln Center. Actually, another Asperger's syndrome warning sign happened there, only we didn't know what it was. We had front row seats to the *Nutcracker*. I was enjoying the performance, until the part when the mice start fighting with swords. Strobe lights began flashing, and when I saw them, I suddenly felt like I was going to faint or actually have a seizure. I didn't know what was happening to me, but I whispered to my mother that I thought I was going to faint. She looked over at me just as my eyes rolled up in my head and I slumped forward. She quickly covered my eyes with her hand and kept talking to me. I didn't pass out, but I nearly did. We never understood what had happened, until I learned what Asperger's syndrome was. Strobe lights affect us folks just like it did that night.

Another fun thing to do was to "attend" red-carpet events at Lincoln Center. Whenever a new performance began, there was a gala opening. If you got there early, you could be right behind the red ropes to see some of New York's rich and famous. It was always lots of fun.

Tavern on the Green and the Plaza Hotel's Palm Court were my favorite places to go. Aside from the elevator-fiasco day, all my other trips to afternoon teas were outstanding. The Palm Court had violins and a harp, and it was very soothing to me. I never had any desire to attend any of the hopping New York nightclubs.

Regular Visits to the World Trade Center

On September 11, 2001, the world witnessed the appalling tragedy of terrorists flying airplanes into the World Trade Center, and the subsequent, shocking fall of both towers. People watched in horror. It was especially profound for me.

From 1986 through 1988, I made regular visits to the World Trade Center and the restaurant Windows on the World. The restaurant was on the 107th floor of the North Tower. I went there with Richard, my former fiancé. I never liked going up so many stories, because aside from the height factor, the one-minute elevator ride was traumatic for me. Here again, my AS issues were rearing their ugly head. By about the eightieth floor, my ears would start popping, and I'd feel like pressure was building in my head. By the time we got to the restaurant level, I'd have a raging headache, which would usually last until the next day.

The hallway leading to the restaurant was very glamorous, lots of mirrors, lots of windows. I didn't want to go anywhere near those huge windows. Of course,

Richard just had to have me by his side, and would grab my hand to drag me over to look out. Granted, it was spectacular, but looking down more than one hundred stories was sickening to me. Then we'd go to the restaurant. As if we were not high enough, Richard always made the reservations in the special area that was raised about twelve feet higher than the rest of the place. There were only a few tables up there. Love must be really blind, because I was so scared, yet went along with this whole thing. The food and service was grand, but all I wanted was out of there. Of course, to get down you had to go on that one-minute elevator ride. All I could think of as I stepped into that miserable thing was that below the floor of the car was a 107-story drop to the bottom. Once we made it safely down, it was great to go outside and look up to the top of the towers. Only by being there and actually seeing them could one appreciate their magnitude.

Watching the attacks unfold on September 11 were deeply profound to me, because I knew those towers well and could envision the terror those poor people felt, who were in the buildings that morning. One thought I'll never get out of my mind is that approximately two hundred people jumped to their deaths from the towers that morning. I couldn't even stand getting near those windows to look down, and they were jumping. I hope they were unconscious before they hit the pavement. I guess they decided falling to their deaths was better than burning to death. Another thing my Asperger mind did was imagine what it was like for the people sitting at their desks, who looked out the windows and saw a passenger airplane coming at them at about 500 mph. Or the people trapped in the elevators once the buildings were hit and on fire. I don't know why I got fixated on all this, but I did. When I would talk about it to others, they would throw their hands up and say they just didn't want to hear it. I still get fixated on it, as I am right now. Okay, I'll stop.

An Outsider in a Class of Six

There were only six other students in my class, and in no time flat they were a group and I was on my own. Of course, I now realize I got in that situation because I probably did things that annoyed them, or I was simply too different. I truly didn't know how to act, other than my version of me. All it did was make me tougher. If I'd known back then that I had Asperger's syndrome, things could have been different. For sure I was the square peg trying to fit in a round-hole world. In a way, I guess I never really cared that I didn't fit in anywhere. I had so many things that I loved to do, and I directed my energy into those. I spent little, if any, time wondering why I didn't fit in.

Obviously learning how to give anesthesia is a complex, intense course of study. That in itself is a major stress. Combine that with having AS and all the negative social interactions to deal with, my adrenaline would be on overload at any given time.

My days would start at 3:30 a.m., when I'd get up, eat, and go over to Roosevelt Hospital to start the day in the operating room. I'd usually get there by five. First I'd check the anesthesia machine to be sure everything was working properly. Then I would draw all the drugs—lidocaine, propofol, succinylcholine, atracurium, ephedrine, propofol, and a 100cc bag made up with phenylephrine. After all that was done, I would go see the patient in the pre-op area. The routine was that you would see your patients the evening before and then make up an anesthesia care plan. This care plan was specific for the type of surgery the patient was having, as well as all of their medical problems. You planned the anesthetic they would receive, including all the dosages calculated for their specific weight.

There were five clinical instructors; and of those, there were two that pretty much hated me and did all sorts of things to make my life miserable. One thing in particular could have cost me not only my career but my life, because I would have ended up in jail. One day, while working with one of the instructors who hated me, I couldn't find a box of fentanyl, which is a controlled substance, a narcotic. I had been assigned to a room doing D&Cs all day, which are quick procedures with a fast turn-over. There had been about fourteen cases that day. I had checked out two boxes of fentanyl. Each box contained ten vials; each vial contained 5cc. I dropped off my patient from the sixth case and returned to the operating room, and the first thing I realized was that my two boxes of fentanyl were missing. There was a little lockbox on top of the drug cart for keeping the narcotics in, but someone had gone into it and taken the boxes. The blood drained out of my head. I started looking around frantically, and my instructor found this most amusing. I realized she had done this, but thought, *Good luck proving it.*

They were ready to start the next procedure, so I had to go check out more fentanyl. On the outside I maintained my composure, but inside, I was freaking out. The nurse, Mabel, who was in charge of the narcotics, was a kind person and really liked me. When I went back to the pre-op area and saw her, I started crying. I told her that my two boxes of fentanyl were missing, and that I thought my instructor had something to do with it. She gave me a hug and instructed me to calm down. She would help in any way she could.

Finally all my cases were done, and I went back to the pre-op area to see Mabel. She had a plan. Since she was getting off duty right then, she said we should go back to the operating room where the fentanyl had gone missing. We went in there and searched every nook and cranny in the room. Then she said we should check the garbage bag that had been in the room. The hospital garbage bags were huge red bags, and by that time they were long gone from the room. They were down in the holding area, waiting to be thrown down the main trash chute. If the bag has already gone down the chute, it would be impossible to get it. We literally ran down the hall to the area with all the big red bags. Mabel grabbed some and I grabbed some. We took them back to that operating room, and one by one opened them and dumped the contents on the floor. All the trash in each bag was alike, because they were from all the operating rooms, so we couldn't differentiate what was from my room. Then Mabel opened the last bag. As she shook out all the contents, out tumbled the two boxes of fentanyl, with all the vials that should have been in them. I burst out crying with relief.

How could someone be so evil to have buried those boxes in the bottom of that bag? They would have ended up in the city dump, and I would have ended up in jail. It took me a long time to get over that, but I realized it was yet another thing to go through because I was different. It was obvious the instructor was not happy that I found those boxes. Her plan failed.

I got extensive clinical experience while earning my master's degree in nurse anesthesia. Between doing our training at Roosevelt and Columbia-Presbyterian Medical Center, we got farmed out to other places for specialty anesthesia. I was sent to Brooklyn for a month to do obstetric anesthesia, which is where I learned about Hasidic Jews. The whole area around the hospital was heavily Hasidic, and it was a culture unto itself. The men all wore long black wool coats and hats, and two long curls hung from under their hats by their ears. Women shaved their heads and wore scarves. I also found out that I wouldn't get waited on in one of their restaurants, because I wasn't one of them. It was a real culture shock.

The next destination was a hospital out on Long Island, or as the locals there called it, Lawnguyland. We had to work a month there on open-heart anesthesia. This is where I found out just how much I was being harassed by my instructors back at the home site. It was a Friday afternoon, the third week into the month there. I kept hanging around, offering to do cases long after my day was officially done. The chief anesthetist came over to me to ask why was I still there. I said that I wanted to get more cases, because I knew I needed as many as I could get. He looked puzzled and asked what I meant. I told him that several of my instructors (the ones that hated me) would frequently say I wasn't doing such a good job.

He burst out laughing. "You have got to be kidding me. Anita, you are one of the best students to ever rotate through here. All the anesthesiologists are saying it, and I can see your abilities. You are the last one from your group to be here, and you can run circles around them. Get that thought out of your head, because you are an excellent anesthetist."

That really made my day. I left then and had a wonderful weekend.

Graduation finally came, and I was on my way to the next goal, taking my CRNA board exam. That came before I knew it. I had gone to Pittsburgh, Pennsylvania, for a three-day review class, traveling on Amtrak with my mom. That was my first train ride. I could have done without the Horseshoe Curve in the Allegheny Mountains.

As the train takes a long loop around, the conductor tells the passengers to go look out the window at the 1,000-foot drop down to the lake below. Just what I wanted to look at. We had to go past it again on the way home.

Years later I attended a course relating to work. It was at a hotel in Chicago. As luck would have it, one of my clinical instructors from college—the one who was my favorite, and who had believed in me throughout my two years there—was also attending. We met for dinner the first night in the restaurant in the hotel. I was relieved, and yet angered, by what she told me during our meal.

She brought up how badly I had been harassed by some of the clinical instructors during the program, and informed me that I had immediately been selected as *the one* from the first day of the program. Apparently, each year those instructors would zero in on a particular student to harass during their entire course of study. They did the same exact things to each of them. Gayle said she could pick out which student would be targeted, because it was always someone who was different. She told me I shouldn't take it personally, and that I had been very strong to take it like I did. She then told me about a student who had been there more recently. She wasn't as strong emotionally as I was. The woman was in her late twenties, divorced with a young daughter. She was *the one* in her class. Those same instructors were on her case, and one day she went into bathroom of the locker room and tried to kill herself. She might have succeeded if someone hadn't happened to go in there and found her unconscious on the floor. That news greatly saddened me. All that because she was different.

Passing the CRNA Exam

The day I graduated from Columbia with my master's degree in nurse anesthesia was a happy one indeed. Passing my CRNA board exam and having that letter of congratulations in my hand felt awesome. Now it was time to get a real job!

Stopping by Bloomfield High School

Just after graduating from Columbia University, I returned to my hometown of Bloomfield for a week. One day I happened to be driving past the high school, and I suddenly just pulled over, parked my car, and went in. As I walked up the front steps, all the unhappy memories flooded into my head. I recalled the endless laughter directed at me, the never-ending torment from my peers, and the mental and physical abuse I sustained during my three years there. It didn't stop me from proceeding up the stairs and into the building. Once inside, I headed down to the administration area. Arriving at the office, I said that I had graduated from the school back in 1977, and was wondering if any of the same teachers were still there. It turned out that the man who had been my Spanish teacher was now the principal. The secretary went into his office to see if he had time for a visitor.

He came out to greet me, and seemed very glad to see me. He took me into his office, asking how I'd been since I graduated. I told him I had just graduated from Columbia with a degree in nurse anesthesia. He sat back in his chair a bit, a strange smile on his face. He asked me if I was aware that when I was in high school, I had been in the lowest section in each of my grades. He stated that I had been a real enigma to all the teachers, because they knew I was really smart, but in my own way and on my own terms. He asked why I never applied myself to do better. I answered that I thought school was very boring and a complete waste of my time. I hated every minute I was there. I had much more important things to do, and didn't want to be forced to learn stuff that I saw as worthless. I was there for over an hour, and we talked and laughed at what I was like back then. He said he felt very proud of my accomplishments.

I was glad I had made that stop, because it was like a closure for me. It helped close the wounds that were left from those high school days. The kid who had been the focus of three years of ridicule was now an Ivy League graduate with a master's degree. I felt like I had the last laugh.

Chapter 5:

Employment: Struggling with Asperger's Syndrome in the Workplace

A large number of people with Asperger's don't work, and collect disability. That's a really sad fact of Asperger's syndrome, one that I hope changes over time. I believe it will, as more people are formally diagnosed and come to realize they are protected under the Americans with Disability Act. As long as someone is doing his job well, the employer and other employees need to get over it that the person is different. I like big, complex cases with very sick patients, and that is what I regularly get assigned to do. An employer would be hard-pressed to fire me because of anything to do with my job performance, because my skills and years of experience are a great asset to patients. All of my work-related problems have stemmed from someone in authority who instantly disliked me, and then made it his mission to try to get rid of me. What I find most amusing is that just about every one of them is no longer at his job, for one reason or another. And if they are still at their job, some ill-fated thing has happened to them. Perhaps they should have just ignored me, and their lives would have remained the same. I believe it's their punishment for harassing someone who was simply born different.

Asperger's on the Job

I am a different person because of things that happened at jobs in the past, and now that those things are over and done with, I'm much more relaxed. These were experiences that only another person with Asperger's, or a support person, could truly understand. People with Asperger's normally have a degree of anxiety, but my level was constant and heightened. Fortunately, I've always been able to compartmentalize, and shut out distractions when I'm going into the operating room to do anesthesia. I really don't know too many people who, after a boss has told her she's on the verge of being fired, could go right into the operating room and do a case, simply tuning out what had just been said. I'm quite sure the boss did that hoping I'd mess up, and then I really would be fired. I'm sorry I disappointed him. That's life.

In order to tell that story, I need to go back a number of years to a place I used to work. The names will all be changed, but they will know who I am referring to. They will be in a rage, I'm sure, but perhaps they should go look in the mirror and ask themselves what I had ever done to them to warrant their behavior to me. The answer is, nothing—except for being different and not fitting in with their idea of what's normal. That's what did it. I'm excellent at what I do, but because I have Asperger's syndrome, I know that how I say something or what I say is sometimes taken incorrectly. They might not like what I said, but they couldn't deny that I'm an excellent anesthetist.

I am truly amazed at how much trouble one person in particular generated, on a daily basis, as she was on a nonstop mission to bring me down. She'd even spend her weekends plotting out her next scheme. I see this as mental illness, to be totally consumed by someone. This woman—whom I'll call Betty—made up lies about me, grossly exaggerated and distorted things I said, sought out coworkers and superiors to badmouth me, and did everything humanly possible to take me down. The worst part of it was that she had an enabler, a person who listened to her and actually believed her lies. Most other people I worked with knew she was lying, and frequently they would come up to me to tell me what her latest one was. After my boss received the letter from my neuropsychologist, confirming that I have Asperger's, I told him he *really* needed to make her stop harassing me. He did speak to her, and she cooled it for a few months. A coworker even came up to me one day and said, "Wow, they must have said something to Betty. She hasn't made up any lies about you for a few weeks. She just stopped, cold turkey. We all figured someone must have said something to her to stop it."

That's pretty sad, that it was so bad that people noticed when it stopped. But I blame her enabler in part, whom I'll refer to as Mike.

The Beginning of Ten Years of Being Bullied in the Workplace

This was a number of years ago, and I had been at my new job for a week. I needed hay for my horses, but I was going to be at work for fourteen hours that day and would not be able to go purchase any. The plan was that my mom would drive me to work and then take my truck over to the feed store and get the hay. And that's just what we did. There was only one problem: When I was getting out of the truck, I didn't know that Betty was watching me. About a week later, several coworkers asked me if it was true that I'd lost my license because of a DUI. I don't drink, and I'm very much against drunk driving. To say I was shocked is an understatement.

"Where on earth did you get that from?" I asked these people. It was unanimous: Betty. Betty had just made up her first in an endless string of lies about me. I was floored. I went to speak to my boss about it, to which he replied, "Well, Betty is like that, and everyone knows it."

That didn't help me. Four years later, that rumor was still going around about me. I corrected people when they asked me about it, but how many people didn't ask me and believed it? That deeply troubled me, because I'm so against drunk driving.

Several months later, I had to get a wisdom tooth pulled out. I took off a Wednesday to get that done. The next day, three people asked me if it was true that I'd had artificial insemination. I asked them where they had heard that, and just as I expected, they all replied, "Betty." I sent my boss an e-mail about it, and he said again, "Well, you know she's like that." So that was supposed to make it all right.

Over the next eleven years, Betty constantly harassed me. I won't bore you with the mundane stuff, mostly petty things that she tried to turn into catastrophes. She'd make things up, or take something I'd said or done and contort it or add on to it, making mountains out of molehills. I'm guessing she thought that even if she couldn't get me fired, sooner or later I'd get fed up and leave on my own. One thing she never figured out about me is my unwavering perseverance. It is one of my most valued traits. Plus, why would I give her the satisfaction of quitting and making her happy? She had to be one of the most miserable people on earth. You could see it written all over her face. Who else besides a thoroughly miserable person would spend all her time obsessing about another person who had never done anything to them? I'm sure she was a bully in school, because a leopard doesn't change its spots. And, to exercise the First Amendment of freedom of speech, I'm sure it all boiled down to the fact that she was violently jealous. If you knew what she looked like, you'd understand. Her enabler, Mike, never figured out that the female factor of jealousy was the driving force behind all her actions. Take, for example, when I got my official diagnosis of Asperger's syndrome. Betty would laugh about it and say to people, "Anita actually thinks she has Asperger's syndrome." The way she said it, it sounded like this was a good thing. So she was even jealous that I have Asperger's syndrome.

Thrown out of My Comfort Zone

I will talk about several things that Betty did. One thing in particular, I didn't even find out until three years later that she was responsible for it. I can't imagine why I didn't see it was her at the time, but I think I was so shocked, I simply was blinded.

Several years earlier, I started working with one of the surgeons— I will call him Dr. Jeffrey—on a regular basis, because I loved doing his cases and he loved me doing them. He was a bariatric surgeon, who did all the laparoscopic gastric bypasses and laparoscopic gastric bandings. The first time I worked in his room, I realized I had never seen anyone handle the scopes like he did, especially considering the patients were a wee bit large. After working together a few more times, we both really clicked.

He liked the special way I did those cases, waking the patients up like they had never even had surgery or anesthesia, and I liked working with such an excellent surgeon. Plus, he had a very specific routine. Everything was exactly the same for each and every case. An Aspie's dream. I still didn't know at the time that I had Asperger's, but I knew I thrived on routine.

I had been working Mondays, Wednesdays, and Fridays for many years, but eventually Dr. Jeffrey talked me into changing my schedule so I could do all his cases. So I changed it to Mondays, Wednesdays, and Thursdays, from 7 a.m. to 8 p.m. If he had any cases on Tuesdays, I would come in to do those and then leave. I did that for a year and a half, all of his cases, every single one of them. It was always the same staff in the room, the "official team." We had tons of fun. Obviously we were all serious about the job at hand, providing the patients with world-class care. But the conversation was always lively and entertaining.

One of the highlights was when Dr. Jeffrey took on a general surgeon to train to be a bariatric surgeon. I'll call this young surgeon Dr. Jackson, because that's where he was from. It was a pleasure to watch his transformation over the next year, becoming a bariatric surgeon and do everything exactly like his mentor. I sort of felt like a mother hen watching over her young. He was a great guy, and I was so proud of him when he was done. Unfortunately, he ended up going to another hospital to work. I had been looking forward to doing the anesthesia for his cases. But actually, I wasn't there for the last few months of his training. Dr. Jeffrey had thrown me out of his room. Permanently.

I'm going to spoil the suspense by first telling you that Betty was responsible, only I didn't find this out until three years later. What I did know was that I hadn't done what Dr. Jeffrey accused me of. As I stood there looking at him screaming at me, I literally could not believe my eyes or ears. It was a devastating experience, very emotionally damaging and humiliating. It's hard to describe the feelings I experienced that day and for months, actually, years, to come.

When you have Asperger's, doing a job that has routine suits you just fine. You thrive on it. Well, I was thriving on Dr. Jeffrey's room. We all worked together like a finely tuned watch. One of my proudest moments as an anesthetist happened right there in that room. For months, Dr. Jeffrey had been mentioning a patient he'd be doing who weighed over six hundred pounds. As the surgery date came closer, he'd bring it up more and more. Finally, it was the morning of the big day. I had not yet met the patient in the pre-op area, when Dr. Jeffrey walked down the hall toward me. I'd never seen him looking so serious.

"The surgery and anesthesia have to be flawless for this case," he said.

"As it always is," I replied.

And, of course, the case went with flying colors. When I woke the patient, he sat up like he never even had anything done. The patient was smiling, talking, laughing. Dr. Jeffrey was so happy, he told the circulating nurse to go to the front desk to get a camera and take a photo. When she returned with the camera, Dr. Jeffrey, the patient, and I posed with our arms around one another. Right at that moment, I was about to burst with excitement and pride. Dr. Jeffrey was proud of me; and I was proud of him, because only a surgeon with outstanding surgical skills could have pulled that off.

I was really thriving on the routine of our room. Perfect for an Asperger person. Betty was in a constant rage that I was in that room all the time. She regularly questioned the anesthesiologist who was the chairman of our department, why is Anita in that room all the time? She was told over and over that Dr. Jeffrey wanted me in his room, that was why I was there. It ate away at her. She even would go up to Dr. Jeffrey and try to start some sort of trouble for me. When I'd go on vacation, she'd ask to be assigned to his room. When I would return the following week, I would hear all the tales of her week in that room. Why I didn't figure out what was about to happen is beyond me.

It was a typical day for us, two laparoscopic gastric bypasses followed by a lap band. The first case had been a tough one for Dr. Jeffrey. The patient had had a lot of prior abdominal surgery, thus had a lot of scar tissue to contend with. We had just wheeled the patient into the recovery room, when Dr. Jeffrey came over and said he needed to talk to me. I was puzzled and somewhat anxious all of a sudden. He looked very strange. He walked us over to a corner so we were out of direct view of everyone. He then burst out yelling at me.

"I don't *ever* want you to step foot in my room! I know you called administration on me!"

I was stunned. I had absolutely no idea what he meant. "What are you talking about?" I asked.

"I know you called the administration's hotline to say that I'm a racist," he shouted.

"I didn't do it, I didn't do it," I insisted. I even swore on my mother's life that I didn't do it. He wasn't buying it. He just kept ranting and raving that he knew I'd done it and he couldn't ever trust me. I had betrayed him, on and on.

I was so flushed with adrenaline, I was scalding hot from head to toe. Everything seemed to be echoing, and I thought I was going to faint. I remember yelling back at him that there were a lot of things I could have said about him, but being a racist wasn't one of them. That would never have occurred to me. He finally stormed out, and I stood there dazed for a few moments. I then turned and rushed into the anesthesia office, where several of the anesthesiologists were sitting. I started blurting out what had just happened, only to realize everyone seemed to know already. One of them took me aside to tell me that earlier in the day, Dr. Jeffrey had informed them that he had just returned from administration, where he had been read the riot act because of a call on the hotline, allegedly from me, stating that he was a racist. I was shaking so badly, I could barely speak. I told this anesthesiologist that I had never made the call and it wasn't me. Still, it went around the whole building like wildfire that Dr. Jeffrey had thrown me out of his operating room. Everyone was as shocked as I was.

So here I was, so set in my daily routine of that room and all the particulars, and now I'd be assigned to anything and everything. It threw me for a loop. I was switching from doing the same thing every week to doing something different every day, all day. Here's where having Asperger's really affected me. Sure, I had twenty years of experience doing all kinds of serious cases, but it was the routine that I had gotten so used to. The best way I can describe is that I just felt lost. Empty inside. To make matters worse, the next day I was in the recovery room checking in a patient, and Dr. Jeffrey walked up behind me and whispered in my ear, "I know you called the hotline." I didn't even respond.

I was totally bewildered by the whole event. I knew I hadn't called the hotline, but Dr. Jeffrey was totally convinced I had. Three years later I found out who did call.

One day, I was talking to someone in the operating room about my nearly twenty-four years as an anesthetist and all the types of cases I'd done. The other person suddenly said, "It's really a shame what Betty did to you to get you out of Dr. Jeffrey's room." The individual proceeded to tell me that Betty had called the hotline and pretended she was me. She went on to say that it was too bad Dr. Jeffrey kicked me out, because I was so talented for those bariatric cases.

So there it was, the real reason I got kicked out. I got my usual adrenaline flush. A coworker happened to come in then to give me a break. I needed to get out of that room. I went into the doctor's lounge, and Dr. Jeffrey's physician's assistant was there. I was glad to see him, and asked him to give a message to Dr. Jeffrey for me. I was so angry about what Betty had done, my voice shook. I told him what I had just learned, and to please relay it to Dr. Jeffrey. He could see how irate I was, and he assured me he'd tell Dr. Jeffrey.

I just couldn't imagine how I didn't see at the time that Betty was behind the whole thing. I would have demanded the administration play the tape to prove it wasn't my voice.

I found another "comfort zone" with the hospital's chief of neurosurgery, Dr. Michaels. He liked how I did my anesthesia, and I liked his routine. I love doing complex cases, like aneurysm clippings, brain tumors, and big spine cases. And, of course, we always have the same staff in the operating room, handpicked by Dr. Michaels. It was just like the good old days!

Unfortunately, something happened in Dr. Michael's room that is another display of what bullying, harassment, and a hostile work environment is like for an Asperger's syndrome person.

In chapter 14, about auditory and visual senses, I discuss the surgeon who played extremely loud music. I had to request never to work with him. The nurse involved in the following incident worked in the neurosurgery suite, and she knew I would not work with that particular surgeon because I couldn't tolerate the loud music. She also knew I have Asperger's syndrome. I'll refer to her as Annie.

For about two weeks leading up to the incident, once a case was underway, Annie would go out of the operating room into the sub-sterile room where the big radio/CD player was and put on her favorite station. That station, unfortunately, played music that featured either high-pitched female singers or heavy metal. As an anesthetist, obviously I am unable to leave the operating room. I'm literally trapped in the room. When Annie would come back into the OR, I'd politely ask her to put on something soft that I could tolerate. She would go and do it, but I could see she was annoyed.

One day, Annie went out to put on her favorite station, as usual. I decided to see if I could stand it, but within minutes I got a headache and felt physically ill. It was only 7:30 in the morning, and it was going to be a long day in that room. I couldn't stand it another second. Right then, Steve—a senior level neuro nurse—walked in, and Annie went out for a coffee break. I asked Steve to kindly put on the soft station. He did. Annie returned fifteen minutes later, and the second Steve walked out of the room, she put her station back on.

I went over to her. "Annie, did you just change the station?"

"Yes, I did," she replied, indignantly. "There was static on that other station and I'm *not* going to listen to static."

"Annie," I said, "you know I have Asperger's syndrome. You know I cannot tolerate that kind of music with Asperger's."

Her response floored me. "Well, that's just tough. I'm not going to listen to static."

"Okay, then," I said. "Go call Dr. Anderson and tell him to get another anesthetist in here to take over the case."

I truly thought she'd back down at that point and just go change the station. Instead, she very happily picked up the phone, called Dr. Anderson, and told him my request. Five minutes later, another anesthetist came in to take over. After giving my colleague my report about the patient and the case, I informed Dr. Michaels that I was leaving—and why I was leaving.

Several hours later an operating room nurse walked up to me and said she had heard about what happened in Dr. Michael's room. She then went on to tell me that about two weeks earlier, she had overheard Annie telling someone that she couldn't stand me and wanted me out of that room. Annie said she knew I wouldn't work in the other surgeon's room because of the music, so she knew just how to get rid of me.

So she used my sound sensitivity to her advantage, to get me out of her room.

What Happens When You Receive a Pornographic E-mail from a Superior

This was a very unusual situation. The downward spiral started after I made a formal complaint about a staff anesthesiologist who had a screaming fit at me in the recovery room in front of about fourteen people. Several months prior to that, this same man, whom I'll refer to as Dr. Smith, had sent me a pornographic video. I intensely disliked Dr. Smith, and everyone there knew it. There were many reasons I felt that way, and actually, I wasn't the only one.

Dr. Smith knew I loved horses, and one day he told me he was going to e-mail me a horse video he thought I'd like. I considered that strange, as he knew how I felt about him. That night when I got home from work and checked my computer, sure enough, there it was. In the subject line was "what an exotic horse." I thought it would be some rare breed, clicked on it, and then sat back in shock. He had sent me a porn video. A man and a woman were on a horse having sex, first vaginal and then anal sex. I was repulsed and very upset. The next day, Dr. Smith asked how I enjoyed his message. I told him I thought he was pathetic and walked away. I didn't act on the incident immediately, mainly because it was very embarrassing, but also because my bosses were all male. If we'd had one female superior, I would have made a complaint right then.

Several months later, Dr. Smith made that big scene in the recovery room, right in front of the patient's surgeon and several staff members, including other anesthetists from our own department. True, Dr. Smith had a history of violent outbursts, but I wasn't going to take it, especially after the porn video he sent. I wrote up both incidents and handed them in. I also forwarded the lovely video as well and then waited to hear something from them. Them being the chairman of our department and one of the anesthesiologists on the grievance committee. A month went by. Nothing. Another month went by. Nothing. Then early one morning, just as I was getting ready to go to the operating room to start a case, I was taken into our little anesthesia office by Mike, the same Mike I spoke of earlier, Betty's enabler. Our chairman, whom I'll call Dr. Hunter, was also there. Mike was one of the anesthesiologists. They were about to tell me I was on the verge of being fired.

Several days earlier, I was doing a case when one of the operating room staff mentioned that he had heard the anesthesia department had hired a new nurse anesthetist, a recent graduate. He had known her when he worked in the ICU at another hospital in a neighboring state, when she was still a nurse. He proceeded to tell everyone in the room, and there were about eight of us, this individual's colorful past. While she was a student at a big university, she got involved with the basketball coach. He was a very prominent figure, and also was married with five children. As always happens with these affairs, they were found out, and the coach lost his job, along with his seven-figure contract. It was public record, as it had been in all the media, including on the TV, newspapers, etc., the guy telling us said. You can find the whole story online.

That evening at dinner, I told my friend Lori, another nurse anesthetist, what I had learned about the new nurse, Cathy. Lori jumped up from the table where we were eating in the lounge, and ran over to a computer to Google Cathy's name. There it was, a big photo and a write-up about the affair. Lori was excitedly reading it when several other anesthetists came into the lounge. They went over to see what had her so enthralled. So they saw it too, Cathy's photo and the big article. Doubtless, they would go and tell more people.

So now I'm standing in our little anesthesia office, which is within the operating room area, right next to the front board where everyone congregates to keep track of the cases in progress and see what's still to go. Despite the door to the room being closed, if one talks loudly enough, people out in the hallway can hear you. Dr. Hunter and Mike both accused me of spreading gossip about Cathy, and warned me that if I ever did anything like that again, I would be fired. They said Cathy was very upset at what people were saying, because she had wanted a new start here, and didn't want anyone to know about her past. I told them where I had heard about it, and that eight other people had been in the OR, hearing the same story. I also stated that Lori was the only person I had told, and she was the one who went on the computer to Google Cathy's name. The conversation kept going around and around in circles, with Dr. Hunter and Mike saying that I was the one who had told Lori, so it was my fault. At one point, Mike stated that I had "tainted" Cathy. I nearly burst out laughing.

"She did a pretty good job of tainting herself," I said. "Getting involved with a high-profile university coach who's married with five kids is courting danger, because sooner or later it's going to come out. She tainted herself."

Dr. Hunter also made the statement that I hadn't liked it when Betty did it to me for ten years, which was acknowledging that he'd known what she was doing, yet no one had stopped her. As I was standing there listening to them, it suddenly occurred to me that they were making much more fuss about Cathy than they had about the two formal complaints I'd filed against Dr. Smith.

They were done with threatening me about getting fired. I walked toward the door, but then spun around and said, "It's absolutely amazing, absolutely amazing, that you think it's so important that I told Lori about Cathy, but you don't think Dr. Smith's sexual harassment is important. His screaming episode was bad enough, but the porn video was blatant sexual harassment." I do believe I made my voice go up quite a number of decibels with that statement, so much so that I'll bet everyone standing outside the door heard exactly what I said. Dr. Hunter pretended he didn't know what I was talking about, and said he'd look into the matter. I left the room and went to the neurosurgery suite to do my case. I shut it all out of my head and just went in with a clear mind. I didn't allow myself to think about it all until I got home that night.

The first thing I did when I got on my computer later, was e-mail the porn video clip to Dr. Hunter, so he couldn't say he never saw it. Two months earlier I had e-mailed it to Dr. Allen, the one on the grievance committee. I cannot believe Dr. Allen never showed it to our chairman. In any case, now Dr. Hunter could see it firsthand, in all its glory.

A few weeks went by, and I didn't hear anything. Then, one day in the early evening, I saw Dr. Allen walking toward me.

"I need to talk to you about the complaints you handed in about Dr. Smith," he said. "We talked to Dr. Smith about both of your complaints, and he said that he never raised his voice at you in the recovery room. He also he said that you asked him to send you the video."

"You've got to be kidding me," I replied. "First, did you ask the surgeon who was present in the recovery room when Dr. Smith was screaming at me? Second, *everyone* here knows I can't stand Smith. Just the sight of him makes me sick. So why would anyone think for one second that I would have asked him to send me that video. I don't watch porn, never did, never will. So in light of all that, why in God's name would you think I asked him to send me that video?"

Dr. Allen just repeated himself. "Well, we asked him, and he said he didn't raise his voice to you and that you asked him to send the video. And no, we didn't ask the surgeon who was present, because we asked Dr. Smith and we believe him."

Now I saw what I was up against. I knew, without a doubt in my mind, that the threat of being fired was retaliation for making the complaints about Dr. Smith. Dr. Smith had angry outbursts at many others, all of whom wrote up official complaints about him. The complaints were always swept under the rug, so his behavior was actually tacitly encouraged. He would yell at a student right in the pre-op area, in front of the patient, their family, and the staff. He would call a nurse an idiot, or some other demeaning thing, demoralizing the nurse and scaring the patient.

For the next several months, Dr. Smith and I were not assigned to work together, not until the Friday before Memorial Day. I called the OR control desk the night before to find out what I was doing on Friday. When they said Dr. Smith was my staff anesthesiologist, my adrenaline started pumping. I hardly slept all night. I knew there would be problems, but I didn't know just how big they would be.

Being anywhere near Dr. Smith was an emotional strain for me. I was hoping just to get through the day without incident, but that didn't work out. We got into a verbal exchange that had him storming out of the room. I later told Dr. Allen about the event; he said he would talk to Dr. Smith to get his side of the story. Gee, I wondered who he was going to believe. I was looking forward to a three-day weekend, but Saturday evening about seven thirty, my phone rang. It was Dr. Allen calling. He told me Dr. Aaron, one of the other anesthesiologists from the group, was also on the phone, so we could have a three-way conversation.

"We have a very critical situation on our hands," he said. "Dr. Smith wants you fired. He's sent all of us, all fourteen anesthesiologists, an e-mail, demanding that you be immediately fired."

My first response was that the whole thing was about retaliation, and also that Dr. Smith had cultural issues with females; in particular, assertive females. Dr. Allen actually agreed with both of my points, but he stated that the only way to rectify the situation was as follows: Dr. Allen wanted me to apologize to Dr. Smith. Nicely. In a soft, subservient tone. I told Dr. Allen that would never happen. There was no way I was going to apologize to Smith, least of all in a "soft, subservient tone."

One of the most memorable things about that conversation, was when Dr. Allen made a statement regarding "breaks." He said, "We don't owe you people any breaks." He was saying that the anesthesiologists don't owe the nurse anesthetists any breaks, like coffee breaks or lunch breaks. I thought it was an extremely ugly thing to say, considering the nurse anesthetists are the ones in the operating rooms all day, every day, doing all the cases that enable the anesthesiologists to collect the big bucks. It also allows them to have days off and to get out early, so they can go out and enjoy the beautiful weather on their yachts. Someone has to be in the operating rooms administering anesthesia, and it isn't the anesthesiologists.

As the following week went on, Dr. Hunter kept after me about apologizing to Dr. Smith. Finally, he told me to just write an apology and he'd give it to Smith. *Okay,* I thought. So I wrote up a two-sentence apology, and the next morning I gave it to Dr. Hunter. He read it and said that if this was supposed to be for real, then I truly spoke another language. He quickly arranged for an emergency meeting with himself, Dr. Aaron, our big boss Mr. Lozaro, and my coworker Lilly. *Now what?* I wondered. During the meeting, Dr. Hunter spoke nicely to me, but *he* wrote up an apology letter, right there in his office, in front of all these people, and forced me to sign it. I obviously had no choice. He also stated that with my Asperger's, I speak a different language that he and others frequently don't understand. He even suggested he was thinking of bringing in a psychologist to help him and the rest of the group understand Asperger's syndrome.

Several months later, Dr. Smith resigned to pursue other interests.

Dr. Hunter did have a psychologist come and meet with him, Mr. Lozaro, and me, and she educated them about what to expect from someone with Asperger's syndrome. At times Dr. Hunter thought I was pulling his leg with the different things I'd say, so he learned that this was how AS people thought and acted, and that it's all for real.

I'm a very "what you see is what you get" kind of person. I'm totally straightforward and direct, and that's what gets me in trouble. I can't help it that my brain is wired that way. To me it's perfectly normal. How can I screen something before saying it, when I perceive it as totally okay to say it?

The Doctor without a Heart

In chapter 8, about my pets, I tell a story about what happened on a Thanksgiving Day years ago to my cats. Anyone who has ever loved an animal can understand the grief from the loss of a pet, but someone with AS takes a harder hit when a pet dies. On Thanksgiving evening, I called in to work to ask if there was any way I could be off the next day, but the anesthesiologist on call stated there were lots of cases on the schedule for the next day, so I'd have to come in. Still, I told him what had happened to my cats.

The next morning I arrived in the operating room at 6:45. The first thing I did was talk to the anesthesiologist on for the day, asking if it was at all possible for me to leave early, because of what had happened the day before and because I felt so much grief. I started to tell him exactly what had happened, that two pit bulls had ripped open a hole in the patio lattice and killed my cats. The instant I said the dogs killed the cats, he laughed and made some comment about a good cat is a dead one. This is someone who goes regularly to church. I told him that he should respect my feelings even if he hated cats, and how about displaying some compassion for me? Again, I made it clear that I'd like to go home a.s.a.p.

What I didn't know was that one of the other anesthetists, Shawn, who was off that day, had come by the operating room to see if we needed him to work. He was turned away by the anesthesiologist, who said there were enough anesthetists for the day. Shawn left his cell number and told the doctor to call him if he was needed at any time.

At about ten thirty I found out that Shawn had stopped by and wanted to work, but was turned away. I called his number, but there was no answer. I left a message. I tried calling him a number of times, leaving a message each time.

The following Monday I saw Shawn. He told me he had called the anesthesiologist at about two thirty to say he could come in, but again the doctor told him he was not needed. If Shawn had come in, he would have replaced me and I could have left. I then looked for the anesthesiologist to ask him why he'd told Shawn not to come in when he'd known I so desperately wanted to go home. When I confronted him, he got nervous and stated that when Shawn called him, he made the decision that Shawn wasn't needed, that it wasn't worth it for Shawn to come in. Well, my shift was until eight that night, and I would have been very grateful to have left any time before then.

Anonymous Evaluations in the Workplace

Years earlier, I worked at a big medical center in the Midwest. It was a trauma/transplant/burn center, one of the top-rated in the country. My level of skills as an anesthetist were quickly recognized, and I was soon doing all the big, complex cases, like liver transplants, burns, brain tumors, aneurysm clippings. What was also quickly recognized, by the chief anesthetist, Wendy, was that I was different. Strangely, the first time I met her, I got a bad feeling in the pit of my stomach. I'd eventually see why I felt that way.

As time went on, Wendy started saying to me, when I was alone with her, that I didn't fit in. She wouldn't beat around the bush. She'd just bluntly say, "You don't fit in here. Why don't you leave?" I learned one day that she went on a campaign to sway others to her side. I stayed there almost seven years. A lot of interesting things happened along the way.

One of the biggest things was a year into my employment, I learned that all the anesthetists were evaluated by an anonymous evaluation system. What this entailed was that each day you worked, whoever was your staff anesthesiologist for the day would fill out an index card about you, your work, and anything they'd like to write. Best of all, they didn't have to sign their name on it, because it was all supposed to be anonymous. So no matter what anyone wrote about you, you would never know who wrote it. At the end of each year, the cards for each anesthetist were compiled and printed up on a multipage evaluation. That's when you would see all the comments that were made all year. You would not be able to challenge anything, because you never were allowed to know who wrote what.

I'm sure you can already guess where this would go for an anesthetist who has Asperger's syndrome, with deficiencies in social functioning. For the first year, I was never even told that they had this system, or any system, for that matter. One day I was called into one of the anesthesiologist's office to "go over my annual evaluation." I didn't know what she was talking about, but I soon found out. This particular doctor was in charge of reviewing the evaluations with each individual. She also was someone I regularly worked with, and she knew the caliber of my work.

She started out by stating that she considered me an outstanding anesthesia provider, and that I did a great job with all the big transplant, burn, and trauma cases. She then added, "Don't pay attention to some of the comments on my evaluation." *What was that supposed to mean?* I wondered. Taking the evaluation from her, I started glancing through the pages. My eyes got rather large. The comments included things like I didn't fit it, a certain person didn't like my tone of voice, didn't like my facial expressions, or lack of them … I couldn't believe it. I simply couldn't believe it. Oh, there were good things written, too, like what an excellent job I'd done on a complex case, how well I'd handled a big trauma, etc. I was floored by the nonclinical comments.

The doctor again told me not to pay attention to all that stuff. "They're writing that stuff because you are different," she said. "Think of it like this. Would you want to be like them? I'd rather be different."

In hindsight, I think she had AS, because she was different. She didn't socialize with the other anesthesiologists, and I was her favorite anesthetist.

It was difficult for me to ignore the personal comments, because I didn't know who had made them. I started looking at everyone, wondering which person had written what. This went on for nearly seven years. One day, one of the anesthesiologists came up to me to tell me that Wendy had been trying to rally everyone to write bad things about me, and telling them I didn't belong there because I didn't fit in. In light of that, I had no misgivings on what happened next.

The Letter That Turned into Pandora's Box

One day I received a thank-you letter from a researcher at the university hospital where I worked. It wasn't simply a form letter, but was really directed to me, and cited all the things the researcher was thanking me for. Apparently, there had been a four-year study that I had supposedly participated in. At the end, I was told to contact the director of the study if I had further questions. I had questions, all right. What was this all about? Little did I know when I picked up the phone to make that call, I was opening a Pandora's box. It would lead to federal agents raiding the anesthesia office to collect the paper trails of the double set of books Wendy and her accomplices were keeping.

I identified myself to the woman who was the director of the four-year study. I stated that I received the letter, and wanted to know what it was all about. She told me that it was the study I'd participated in by filling out a lengthy questionnaire and survey. I told her I had never filled out any such thing. There was a long pause. "But I have it right here in my hands," she said, "with your signature." I drove over there right then, to show her my signature and verify I'd never seen or signed anything. Once she saw my driver's license, verifying my signature, she was visibly upset.

To make a complex story short, Wendy and several other administrative people in the anesthesia office were involved in diverting government funds that were intended for the study. Wendy and her cohorts forged my signature, along with countless other signatures. These were felony counts, because they had defrauded the government. After the Feds raided the office, people lost their jobs and disappeared. All because I picked up the phone to inquire about that letter.

One of the Cruelest Things Anyone Ever Did to Me

The following is one of the worst Asperger moments I've ever had. At the time, I didn't know I had AS, and it left me totally bewildered. Now I know what it was. But how one person could do this to another is still beyond my comprehension.

After my seven years at the "anonymous evaluation" hospital, I started thinking about where I'd like to relocate to. Brandywine, Pennsylvania, was a nice area, so I researched the need for nurse anesthetists there. I contacted a hospital that was looking to hire several and set up an appointment for an interview. From Wisconsin to Brandywine was 1,000 miles, a two-hour flight. I spoke with the chief nurse anesthetist several times, including the night before I flew down there. He talked to me all about the group, the operating room, the kinds of cases they did, the job benefits, salary, the town, real estate, everything. He stated he was very much looking forward to meeting me, and judging from our conversation, he thought I sounded like a good fit for the group.

I do not like to fly in commercial aircraft. Actually, I'm terrified of it. My mother is the same way. So there were the two of us, terrified, flying to Brandywine. I arrived at the hospital for my appointment, and went to the operating room suite control desk where the chief anesthetist had directed me to go. I told the lady at the desk who I was and why I was there. She paged the guy for me. Moments later, he arrived at the desk. I'll never forget the whole experience. He looked at me as if I were from another planet, and then proceeded to act like he had no idea who I was or why I was there. He said he was very busy and didn't have time to talk to me. I stood there in utter disbelief. I couldn't believe my mom and I had just flown 1,000 miles to have someone do this to me. He brushed me off and left me standing there. I can remember watching him walking away from me, not believing my eyes.

I returned to the rental car, where my mom was waiting for me. I got in and just sat in silence for a while. I couldn't even speak. I then started crying and told her what had happened. We sat there for some time. It was totally surreal. The flight home the next day seemed like 10,000 miles long. That experience was beyond horrible.

"Just Act Normal"

Over the years my bosses have said to me, "Why can't you just act normal?" Well, I do act normal, my normal. I like routine. It is my comfort zone. Every now and then I am sent out of the main operating room to another area to do something, like an epidural down in labor and delivery, or an MRI. I go to pieces, so to speak, and I'm vocal about it. I'm being sent out of my comfort zone, and my way of trying to cope with that is to vocalize my unhappiness about it. The other anesthetists, when asked to do the same things, just go do them. I truly cannot help my reactions to things like that. I get upset, and that is my response. Before I knew I had Asperger's syndrome, I didn't understand why I reacted like that when others didn't. Now I know.

Be the Best at What You Do

The most important advice I'll leave you with concerning employment is, simply, be the best at what you do, no matter what that is. Any difficulties you have stemming from your social skills, or lack of them, can be worked out. You can change to some degree, but it is impossible to act "normal." Your brain is wired differently. If problems persist, get outside assistance, whether from the EEOC or an attorney. The Americans with Disabilities Act is there to protect you.

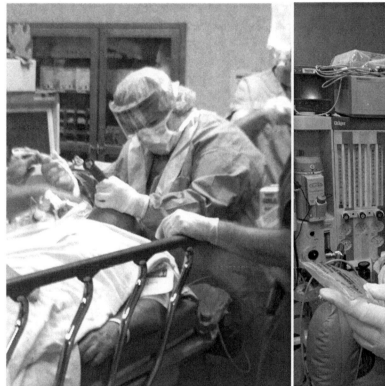

Here I am performing a laryngoscopy, getting ready to intubate a patient.

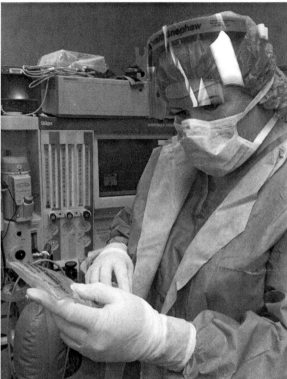

Here I am drawing up drugs before a case.

Chapter 6:

---◆---

A Serious Fall from My Horse

I've been riding horses since age eight, and over the years have had many falls, especially when I was in my late teens and was into jumping. You know it will happen sooner or later, but it's all worth it.

Rescuing a PMU Mare

A number of years ago I had a very bad fall off my horse, Thumper. As I hit the hard, cold ground off a horse that was running at about thirty miles an hour, little did I know that the serious injuries I sustained would be the best thing that had ever happened to me on one the hand, and one of the saddest on the other.

Two years earlier, I had rescued a horse from going to the slaughterhouse. She was a PMU mare. PMU stands for pregnant mare's urine; the horse's urine is used to make hormone replacement drugs for women. She was one of thousands up for rescue, and I rehabilitated her back to health. Thumper was a Percheron; she stood at 17.2 hands and weighed around 2,400 pounds. After successful ground work, I decided to begin riding her. I hired a professional horse trainer, whose expertise was breaking young horses. We did everything by the book, and all was going well until the tenth day. The trainer had ridden Thumper the first seven days, and this day would be my third ride on the horse. I had just gotten on Thumper and rode around my pasture. Suddenly, something spooked her. She leaped into the air, bucking wildly, and then bolted, bucking harder and harder. I managed to stay on for what felt like a long time, but as we neared the fence line, Thumper veered right and I departed left, smashing into the fence post. My titanium helmet sustained a huge dent. My injuries included two pelvic fractures, with my left hip totally fractured, and three fractures of my left shoulder.

A Suspicious Lump on My Shoulder

I was out of work and bedridden for three months, after which I graduated from a wheelchair, to a walker, to crutches, to a cane. Finally I was back to normal, but it was like learning to walk all over again. During my three months in bed, I developed a rash on my arm that wouldn't go away. Once on my feet again, I made an appointment with a dermatologist. While I was pointing at my left arm and telling the doctor about my rash, she was looking at my right shoulder, at an old scar there.

"I want to take a biopsy of this," she said.

"Oh," I replied, "that's an old scar from twenty years ago."

Crinkling her nose, she said, "I don't like the looks of it." She did the biopsy under local anesthesia, and said the office would call with the results in about a week.

No Cards or Calls after My Injury

At my workplace, the chief anesthetist at the time was Betty, the woman who hated me with every fiber of her body. I'm quite sure she took much joy in my accident. Years earlier she had assigned herself the job of being the social coordinator in our department, and orchestrated everything from farewell cakes for departing anesthetists, to baby showers, engagement parties, flowers for sick coworkers, cards, you name it. she was Johnny-on-the-spot for all those things over the years. Of course, as you will guess, she did nothing for me, despite all my fractures and bedridden status. There were three people who did call me. Dr. Anderson, one of the anesthesiologists; Kathy, one of the OR nurses; and Debbie, one of my coworkers. Debbie and Kathy actually came over and visited with me once I was in a wheelchair. Other than those three, no one called or sent a card. My boss sent me a beautiful bouquet of flowers a month after my accident. I had just returned from my first day up and out of the house, which involved a trip to my orthopedic surgeon for follow-up X-rays of all my fractures. By the time I returned home, I was in tears from the pain and could hardly wait to crawl back in bed. Dr. Anderson called then to be sure I would be home, saying the anesthesia doctors were sending me flowers. The bouquet was so beautiful and unusual, I had my mom get my camera for me and I took pictures of it. Months later, I re-created it with silk flowers. Still, not hearing from my other coworkers saddened me, and made for a difficult experience when I finally did return to work and had to talk to them.

No Thanksgiving

My accident happened a week before Thanksgiving. Needless to say, there was no Thanksgiving for me or for my parents, who live with me. I take care of them, and now I was laid up. Not a good situation, least of all for someone with Asperger's who has no friends to help out. As I write this, my mom is in a wheelchair, but thankfully, back then she was still able to get around with crutches. If that had not been the case, I fear what would have happened to me and both of my parents. There was no one to draw upon for help, but somehow we all made it through.

Cancer

It was a beautiful spring morning, and I was getting ready to go outside for a walk when the phone rang. I felt great, and answered the phone quickly, eager to get outside. A soft voice began, "May I please speak to Anita Lesko? This is Dr. Hash ..."

My wonderful mood suddenly plummeted. *Why was the dermatologist herself calling me?*

"I have some bad news," she went on. "That biopsy I took from your right shoulder last week … It's positive for a very rare kind of cancer."

Whatever words Dr. Hash said after that went into an echo. Hearing the word cancer attached to your name has a profound effect on a person. My hearing returned when Dr. Hash said the name of the cancer: dermatofibrosarcoma protuberans.

"We've already scheduled you for surgery a week from tomorrow," she said, "and you will probably need a second surgery to reconstruct the area afterward."

The first surgery was done by a MOHS surgeon. MOHS surgery is the most advanced treatment procedure for skin cancer today. I was his only patient for the day. They had to bring me back to the operating room three times, until he was 100 percent sure all margins were clear and the cancer was all out. The surgery left a gaping wound of about eight inches in diameter, all the way down into the muscle on the top of my right shoulder. The day after the last surgery, a plastic surgeon reconstructed the whole area. Thankfully no skin graft was necessary.

Bullied While Waiting to Go to Surgery

I was in the pre-op area, waiting for my surgeon to arrive to do my reconstructive surgery. My mom was in the little room with me, in a wheelchair. I was terrified, literally terrified, at the prospect of getting anesthesia. Most people are nervous about going to sleep, but it was odd that I was so scared of it, considering I give anesthesia to people every day. It's the feeling of being out of control that I found most daunting. My mom was just as nervous as I was, if not more. The last person I wanted to see right then was Betty, but that's exactly who came walking over to me, all excited. She wanted to share some great news with me. We had worked with another anesthetist, Marcia, whom Betty hated about as much as she did me. Betty told me she finally succeeded in her quest to get Marcia fired.

As she was telling me that she got Marcia out of there, my surgeon came over to greet me. He wanted to check the open wound on my right shoulder. As he lifted the bandage covering it, Betty jumped in front of my mother, stating that she didn't need to see the wound. My mother did want to see it, and I wanted her to see it, but Betty kept moving back and forth in front of her, so my mom never was able to get a look. To this day this angers both my mom and me. Then I had to go to the operating room with Betty still in my face. That was very upsetting. Everyone wants to be with a family member prior to heading into surgery, certainly not with a woman who was on the same mission to get me fired, as she had been on against Marcia.

Unable to Turn My Head

The surgeon had thought he might need to take a skin graft from my thigh if he couldn't close the area, but he was able to do the closure without it. The only catch was that the skin and muscles were pulled so tight, my head was tilted to the right. He had told me pre-op that this would be the case if he didn't do the graft. It would take a month before the area stretched out so that I was able to turn my head to the left.

The Physician Who Punched My Operative Site

The scar was eight inches long and very fragile, because the sutures were pulled so tight. I returned to work a week after the surgery, and I configured a cushion to put over the suture line under my clothing, because I was so scared I would accidentally bump into something with my shoulder. I walked around all day on eggshells. At one point, I was standing in our anesthesia office talking to an anesthesia student, and another coworker was sitting on the couch. One of our anesthesiologists entered the room, looked right at me, and then walked behind me and punched my right shoulder, right on the incision line. In that instant, I thought I was going to faint from the pain, and then I worried that the impact might have torn open the sutures. *Oh my God,* I thought. *What if that happened and I have to get operated on again and get anesthesia again?* I was in tears. What in the world possessed this guy to do that to me? Earlier in the day he had heard me telling someone about my surgery and the suture line, so he couldn't claim he didn't know about it. For that matter, it's hardly normal to punch someone on the shoulder at work. Despite the fact that there were two witnesses to this event who verified that yes, indeed, this guy did that to me, the whole thing was simply swept under the rug and nothing was done about it. That seems to be the usual operating procedure with Asperger's syndrome. Back then I didn't know I had Asperger's syndrome, though.

In conclusion, the fall and subsequent fractures were the best thing that ever happened to me, because they eventually led me to the dermatologist's office and the discovery of my cancer. The sad part was the people who did the cruel things to me. I'll just never understand the need these people have to do mean stuff to someone, whether it's me because I'm different, or anyone else who is their victim.

A few people told me they'd heard Betty saying she was so happy I got cancer. I would not have expected anything less from her.

Chapter 7:

Top Gun Changed my Life

My heart began racing as I heard the voice from the air tower say, "Crow 5-1 cleared for takeoff." The powerful F-15 fighter jet lurched forward as it turned onto the ominous-looking runway, which was covered with thousands of black streaks of burnt rubber from all the jets that had landed on it. I couldn't believe I was actually sitting in the backseat of a multimillion dollar combat aircraft, ready to go on the flight of a lifetime! The pilot, Lt. Col. Mark "Ugh" Lee, asked if I was ready. "Yes, sir!" I replied.

With the brakes on, Ugh eased the throttle forward and lit the afterburners. The massive jet began to feel like a racehorse in the starting gate. I could feel the roar of the two engines, and then Col. Lee bellowed, "Giddy-up!" And off we went! As the jet raced down the runway, I looked over at the treetops, which were rapidly becoming a blur. The tachometer read about 400 knots. I felt the afterburners kicking in, a feeling akin to being punched in the back by a sumo wrestler. I was hyperventilating into my oxygen mask.

At that moment, Lt. Col. Lee pulled back on the stick. We began going straight up to 15,000 feet, pulling about 8.7Gs on the way. It was a feeling of concrete being poured over my whole body. I couldn't move, not even to lift my hand. I was looking at the back of Col. Lee's ejection seat, at the crystal blue sky through the clear canopy, at my G-suit-clad legs ... I was really there! I almost felt like an astronaut, launching into space. Tom Cruise and Kelly McGillis flashed into my mind. If it weren't for them, I wouldn't be in that jet.

Me ready for takeoff in an F-15 at Eglin AFB on December 6, 2002

On a snowy Friday evening in 1997, I was on my way home from work, when I decided to drop in a video store to pick up a movie to watch over the weekend. I happened to see *Top Gun* on the shelf, and for some reason I picked it up. I hadn't seen the movie when it first came out in 1986. I never had any interest in anything military. I didn't even know what *Top Gun* was about, but I soon was on my way home with it. Little did I know that movie would change my life.

As I started to watch the film, I was totally fascinated by the jets landing on an aircraft carrier. I flipped over Tom Cruise as the swaggering Maverick, the fighter pilot with an ego bigger than the ship he landed on. The air combat scenes were astounding! I couldn't believe people were actually that brave to engage in these dog fights, at the speed of sound, upside down! I realized it was only a movie, but I also knew that it existed in real life. I was now on a mission to learn everything I could about military aviation. What an adventure I was about to embark upon. It would become one of the most enriching experiences of my life.

I was living in Wisconsin at the time, and I quickly learned that the Wisconsin Air National Guard housed its F-16 fighter jets at an airport about forty-five minutes away from my home. I can still remember the first time I drove over there on a Saturday to see the jets take off at eight a.m. It was bitterly cold, the usual Wisconsin weather in January. I found a spot to park with a clear view of the runway. I could see the pilots climbing into their jets, and then running up the engines. I was hanging onto a chain-link fence as all six jets taxied by, preparing to take off. When they all raced down the runway in full afterburner, the ground rumbled like an earthquake was splitting it open. The noise was stupendous. I could see the flames from the afterburners coming out of each jet's engines. I was totally overwhelmed, so much so that tears started flowing down my cheeks. (And then froze on my face because it was so cold.) I had a lump in my throat. My hair stood up on my arms. I had never felt so patriotic in my life. Here were America's military forces, real heroes, right before my eyes.

That Saturday morning trek to the airport became my ritual. During the week I would pore over every magazine and book I could find about military aviation. The more I learned, the more I got hooked. I read everything about all the aircraft, right down to what kinds of engines were in each one, how much thrust it had, everything. I learned about all the branches of the military—the Air Force, Navy, Marines, Army, Coast Guard—and how each one played its role in the big picture of how our military functions as a whole. In no time I was subscribing to about ten different magazines, plus looking up endless information on my computer. I began to realize that going once a week to see the F-16s take off wasn't enough for me anymore. I needed to be closer, more involved with this whole military scene.

On a Saturday morning, the mailman delivered my next step. As I sat down at the kitchen table with the usual handful of mail, I noticed an AAA magazine. As I reached for it, it slipped off the table and fell onto the floor, opening up to a page that had an ad for Pensacola, Florida. It wasn't the beautiful sugar-white sand beach or the crystal clear emerald-green water of the Gulf of Mexico that caught my eye, but the picture of the US Navy's Blue Angels flying in a six-jet formation. They were so close to each other, it looked like the jets were welded together. I read the ad and saw that Pensacola was home to this elite precision flying team. Reading on, I discovered there was also the National Museum of Naval Aviation, a world-renowned museum of naval aviation history. It housed a sample of every naval military aircraft since the beginning days of naval aviation. That settled it. I wanted to move to Pensacola, Florida. It seemed like a real adventure to me.

I was working as an anesthetist at a big hospital in Wisconsin. I logged onto the Internet and looked up hospitals in Pensacola. That following Monday, I was on the phone lining up interviews, and asking a Realtor to find me a home and a place to board my three horses. On April 25, 1998, I flew down to Pensacola. Within three days I had secured a job, bought a house, and found a boarding stable nearby. After she found me the house, my Realtor took me to the National Museum of Naval Aviation. I got tears in my eyes as we pulled up, and I saw the huge F-14 Tomcat up on a pedestal in front of the museum. It was hard to believe that such a massive jet could land on the deck of an aircraft carrier. Once inside, I easily understood why millions come to visit the museum, from all over the world. I was excited to learn they offered a volunteer program as well.

Two days later, I got to watch the Blue Angels fly a practice performance at the Pensacola Naval Air Station, their home base. The six F/A-18 Hornets flew formations and maneuvers, the air combat maneuvering skills taught to all Navy fighter pilots. These pilots have nerves of steel, flying only inches apart at speeds of over 400 mph. Seeing this world-famous squadron perform clinched my decision to move to Pensacola. There were no second thoughts.

Several days later I was back home in Wisconsin, preparing to move. One month later, on June fifth, I was landing in Pensacola for good. I had had my horses shipped down a week earlier. Before I even unpacked, I was down at the naval museum signing up to be a volunteer. Many of the volunteers were retired naval aviators, from WWII and Vietnam. They were walking history books. I would sit and listen to their war stories, totally transfixed. I felt honored to get to know these real heroes. It dawned on me one day while listening to a WW II aviator that these stories needed to be shared with all Americans, not just me sitting in on it in a lounge. I decided to officially interview these great people, with a notepad and tape recorder, and put together a book.

At first I began with the volunteers at the museum. To listen as a WW II fighter ace describes the biggest day of his flying career is an enriching experience. Most of them cried at one point or another during their tales. I cried with them. Many had never talked about their war experiences with anyone before opening up to me. It was almost a religious experience. As each one began talking, he was transported back to the time of the actual events, as if he was reliving it right then. And I got to travel with them. Some events were very sad. Some stories were extremely exciting. Each one, though, was intense, as were these people. One of the most heart-wrenching stories was told by the marine who hit the beaches of Normandy on D-Day. He became glassy-eyed as he described that fateful day, what he saw as the ramp of his boat dropped down and the soldiers—part of the third wave—began emerging. The first twenty minutes of Tom Hanks's *Saving Private Ryan* says it all. We went through a lot of tissues during that interview session.

Over a two-year period, I interviewed dozens of our heroes, from Vietnam POWs, Medal of Honor recipients, astronauts, and fighter aces, to Pearl Harbor survivors, Gulf War veterans, and many more. I felt like I went through all those wars right alongside each person. It was an experience every American should have. If a person wasn't patriotic before, you sure would be after meeting these individuals. It made me truly appreciate our freedom, and what so many people have sacrificed to achieve it.

I looked into getting the book published, and soon learned it is no easy process. Either you need to put up thousands of dollars and publish it yourself, and promote it yourself as well; or find a publisher willing to publish it and promote it for you. Not being able to put up the money myself, I had to resort to plan B. I then realized that for a publisher to take you seriously, it is helpful to have a resume of already published works. *Okay,* I thought, *why not write articles for those military aviation magazines that I read?* I had plenty of writing experience from earning my degree from Columbia University. True, those papers were about anesthesia, but the concept of collecting information and writing about it were the same. One problem, though: all the authors of the articles in the military aviation magazines were male. How was I going to be accepted in this environment? But persistence and perseverance are my middle names. Nothing was going to stop me on this crusade!

One of the WW II heroes I had interviewed, Cdr. Roy Whitcomb, lived in Pensacola, and had become a dear friend of mine. I decided to give him some extra glory for his war heroism and send off the story of how he earned his Distinguished Flying Cross to *Naval Aviation News.* I can still remember my excitement when the editor contacted me to say they wanted to publish my article. When I received the issue, it was a thrill to see the story and how beautifully they did the layout of the photos. Roy was equally as thrilled.

From then, I worked at getting one thing published after another. I started out locally with newspapers and journals, and then moved on to bigger magazines like *Air Sports International* and *Wings of Gold.* Eventually, I got published by *Combat Aircraft Magazine,* another international journal of military aviation. I felt like I was finally getting somewhere. I forgot to mention one small aspect, that of photography. All of these articles were accompanied by the photos that I took myself, like of jets going 500 mph, the photo crisp and clear, the jet perfectly centered despite that incredible speed.

Up until I decided to embark on this adventure, I never did any sort of photography. When I needed to take photos, I got a disposable camera. That was the extent of my photography. Now I needed to produce high-quality action photos. I wasn't about to spend years at a local college studying photography. No time for that. Instead, I contacted some of the guys who regularly wrote articles for these magazines and asked what kind of cameras they used. The Nikon F5 was the most consistent answer. I got on the phone and ordered one, though in a state of shock that I was shelling out a few thousand dollars for the camera, and almost as much for the lenses. I hate to read instruction manuals, and will generally struggle with a new item, trying to figure it out myself first. If no luck, then I'll read the instructions. When the Nikon F5 arrived, I had no choice. I needed to go right to the manual, which seemed as thick as a dictionary. It took me almost half an hour just to learn how to load the film. That camera had as many features as the space shuttle, or at least it seemed like it.

***The multiseat spatial disorientation device that
I got a VIP ride in at NAS Pensacola.***

So off I went to try out my new camera at a Blue Angels' practice. When I got the film developed, there were lots of photos of nice blue sky, but no jets. Or there would be parts of jets. Okay, lots more practice necessary. With much determination, I finally started figuring out the camera and the knack of photographing jets going at such high rates of speed. When the photos were good enough, I started submitting them along with my articles for publication.

Blue Angel's # 5 Scott Ind over NAS Pensacola Shermann Field. I was finally getting the quality of photos I needed.

Blue Angel #5 over the Gulf of Mexico during their annual July show over Pensacola Beach. I took this photo from the 12th floor of a condo at show center.

One of the highlights of my new "career" as a military aviation photojournalist, was getting to meet the pilots of the US Navy Blue Angels and watch all the duties the whole team performs in order to put on their heart-stopping, spectacular shows. There are about 120 team members, both officers and enlisted men, who all work tightly together. The one thing that struck me most about all of them was their incredible enthusiasm for their job, their constant striving for excellence, and their pride in being part of the Blue Angels team. The public normally sees the six F/A-18 Hornets and the pilots who fly them. But without everyone else, those jets wouldn't be up there flying!

Me with the U.S. Navy Blue Angels 2000 at NAS Pensacola

Me getting a "flying lesson" with one of the Blue Angels
at their squadron base at NAS Pensacola

Blue Angels display their precision on the ground after their performance

I got to learn what it takes to be selected as a Blue Angel pilot, the winter training they endure, the weekly show cycle that starts every March, and the motto that "The blue jets come first." The team tours the country during the air-show season to about thirty-three locations in the US and Canada, and flies nearly seventy performances.

They bring out nearly 17 million spectators to air shows each season, and they have dazzled over 374 million fans worldwide since their inception in 1946. Their mission is to enhance navy and marine corps recruiting, and to represent the naval service to the United States civilian community, its elected leadership, and foreign nations. They are truly our navy's ambassadors in blue!

I can remember my first visit to the Blue Angels squadron, and the demo pilots all came pouring out of the briefing room. Their energy was simply electrifying!

They all walked by with huge smiles and their fancy blue flight suits. I thought I was the luckiest person in the world to be there and see them up close and personal!

Feel the heat.

I got an assignment to write an article about the 33rd Fighter Wing at Eglin Air Force Base. Now it was time to learn how a fighter wing operates. The wing has two fighter squadrons, the 58th—the Gorillas—and the 60th—the Fighting Crows. Each squadron has about twenty-six F-15 fighter jets. I ended up spending most of my time with the Crows. I also visited the various squadrons that make up the whole wing, and saw firsthand what each one does to operate a fighter wing. I met so many incredible people at the 33rd, each one so knowledgeable, enthusiastic, and loving his and her job. They all made me proud to be an American.

I got to see how the F-15s are serviced from top to bottom; practically disassembled and reassembled; how ejection seats are regularly checked and maintained in the event a pilot needs to exit the aircraft, so he will survive. I saw how missiles are loaded onto the jets; how food is prepared out in field situations, so that 100 percent sanitary conditions are maintained to keep personnel safe and healthy; how the jet engines are removed from the jets and tested in the Hush House; how the fuel tanks and systems in the jets are maintained. I even had the opportunity to look through the night vision goggles that the fighter pilots use. I learned how the pilots train on a daily basis for air combat. These people have nerves of steel and stomachs to match! The challenge to engage in the sorties (missions) they fly is not for the faint of heart. I used to admire what the fighter pilots do up there in the sky, but after I took a flight in an F-15, my admiration took on a whole new perspective!

I got to spend an hour in an F-15 flight simulator, which was operated by the Boeing Corporation and located on Eglin AFB. I had two different instructor pilots, both of whom were retired F-15 pilots. These simulators are used for actual pilot training, and are as realistic as being in a jet. I got to experience flying an F-15! It was quite exciting to push the throttle forward and "accelerate" down the runway. I couldn't believe how sensitive the stick was. Just a tiny movement, and the "jet" was doing something. The instructor pilot told me I was doing so great, the USAF Thunderbirds would be giving me a call! I was doing quite well, until I became fixated on chasing the enemy aircraft they put on the screen for me. I wasn't paying close attention to my altitude or direction, only keeping the enemy in my radar, when suddenly I was heading straight into the Gulf of Mexico at 700 mph. Nice thing about the simulator is I then climbed out of it. Alive. For a minute I had felt like Maverick in the dog-fighting scenes!

The 33rd Fighter Wing had been participating in Operation Southern Watch, enforcing the no-fly zone over Iraq. After 9/11, it also began flying combat air patrols over the nation for homeland defense. They are ready at any moment to respond to the Commander in Chief whenever they are needed. They maintain combat readiness at all times. Each time I visited, I could see the professionalism and seriousness that each person puts into his job. Each role is vital to the successful functioning of the wing.

The most striking thing about each and every military personnel I met, whether enlisted or officer, is that they *love* their jobs! I haven't met too many civilians who *love* their jobs. Not the way these people do. One young man stands out in particular, a twenty-four-year old crew chief for the F-15 squadron. I was out on the flight line for a nighttime launch, with the fighter pilots training with the night vision goggles. This guy was so pumped up, telling me about his job and how he

Me standing by an F-15

loved every minute of it. It was very evident how knowledgeable he was about those jets. He made me feel so proud. Very patriotic.

An assignment to write an article about helicopter training took me to Naval Air Station Whiting Field South in Milton, Florida. Jet pilots always get all the glamour, but I can truly say that I came to deeply admire the skill it takes to fly a helicopter. They put me in the flight simulator that the student naval aviators use for training. We all have seen a helicopter hover. No big deal, right? Wrong! Try using both feet on the rudders, the left hand on a control that increases or lessens power, and the right hand on another control that's for forward/backward/right/left, and work them all at the same time. In my pathetic attempt to learn the art of hovering, I thought of humorist Dave Barry's article on his helicopter-flying lesson, describing it as being like a "crazed bumblebee." Landing on a ship deck at night was even better. The simulator was so realistic, complete with the ship pitching up and down in rough waters. I was hyperventilating while I guided the "helicopter" down aboard the ship. Of course, my instructor pilot, Lt. Allen Cahanding, was helping me through it all, as he sat in the other seat with his hands on the controls as well!

Next came my incredible experience on a magic carpet! The folks at NAS Whiting Field arranged for me to fly in a TH-57 Charlie, one of the helicopters used for training all navy, marine corps, and coast guard helicopter pilots. Lt. Commander Curtis Ford was at the controls for the flight, and he was an excellent teacher, explaining every move and providing an incredible experience. When the helicopter first lifted up, we hovered for a few minutes before taxiing across the flight line, just three feet off the ground. I might have been on a magic carpet! So smooth, with a nice humming sound. Then up we went, to about 700 feet, and over to a training field where nine other helicopters were practicing. More hovering, landing, taxiing. It was more fun than I could ever have imagined! The best part about helicopters is you can put them wherever you want, and do things that are totally unreal. If I had joined the military, I would have wanted to fly helicopters. No question about it. We flew over to where I live, and I took aerial photos of my house. It took me awhile to figure out where my house was, as things look very different from the air!

*Me in the TH-57 Sea Ranger at NAS Whiting Field
getting ready to depart on my helicopter flight*

The helicopter pilots were awesome, real down-to-earth guys. They are humble, and they know the jet jockeys get all the glamour. But I can tell you, it is more difficult to fly a helicopter than a jet. And it takes a lot of courage to fly helicopters into enemy territory, low and slow, a real target for the enemy, to rescue a downed jet pilot. These guys are unsung heroes. Not to mention all the rescues the coast guard does, sometimes at night and over rough seas. Most of the navy and marine corps helo flying is in the demanding environment of at night and over water. Sounds pretty scary to me.

Thus far on my incredible journey, I had met people from all the branches of the military—air force, navy, marines, army, and coast guard. I can say without hesitation that they are all great people. They are America's heroes, going about their duties on a daily basis unnoticed. Whenever I'd say to one of them what an incredible service he was doing, he would simply reply, "I'm only doing my job." They risk their lives for the rest of us. Each and every American needs to stop and think about what we take for granted—our freedom—and realize that it is thanks to these military men and women that we live the lives we do in this great country.

An exciting photo to shoot.

Once we reached 15,000 feet, Lt. Col. Lee rolled the F-15 upside down for a bit. That was heart-stopping, as the jet felt as if it were sinking down in a free fall. I momentarily forgot that he'd told me during the briefing that he was going to do this. I was looking down at the ground way below. It is quite the luxury to have that clear canopy to look out at everything. After we rolled right side up, I felt some strange physiological reactions. My legs felt hot, and a pins and needles sensation prickled all over them. I was a bit disorientated, or perhaps it was simply shock that I was really in the backseat of a fighter jet. Not too many civilians ever get such an opportunity.

One vision that I'll hold forever in my mind is seeing Lt. Col. Lee up there in the front seat, his elbows resting on the canopy ledge, the profile of his helmet and oxygen mask, the blue sky, the gleam of the sun on the canopy. It was surreal. I felt like I was in heaven. I guess you could say I was. I had dreamed of this flight for seven years, but it always seemed like an impossible dream. Yet here I was flying at 0.9 Mach with one of the best fighter pilots in the whole world, in one of America's superior fighter jets. This was one of the most exciting adventures of my life.

I'd like to thank Tom Cruise and Kelly McGillis for playing in *Top Gun*. Those two flights were the pinnacle of all my military adventures, but meeting all the people along the way, the POWs, astronauts, war aces, fighter pilots, bomber pilots, cargo plane pilots, helo pilots, Blue Angels, enlisted personnel … That was the most enriching experience of my life. Sometimes I feel like I have become a walking history book, having experienced so many things through the words of everyone I've interviewed.

***This is one of my best shots, capturing the
USAF Thunderbirds in their famed Calypso Pass.***

Chapter 8:

<hr>

All of My Animals: My Best Friends

I realized at an early age that I have a unique ability to communicate with animals. I have always considered this a gift, and I truly treasure this ability. The other side of the coin, though, is that when one of my animals dies, it's a far deeper loss to me than it might be for other people. That said, I'd rather go through those rough times than never experience the joy and happiness that my furry friends continually bring me. Nothing can relax me better than spending quiet time with them. They accept me unconditionally. They're nonjudgmental, they don't bully and harass me, they don't care how I look. Simply, they just love me for myself.

Animals are drawn to me like a magnet. Somehow they sense that I am different. Even wild animals like raccoons and hawks will come by me when I'm outside on my farm. Raccoons are nocturnal animals, except the ones that live behind my horse barn. There are four of them, and when they hear me, they will come out, even in the middle of the day, and follow me around. One in particular, whom I've named Honey Coon, will sit next to me on a hay bale in the walkway of the barn. The raccoons will follow me back up to the house, and frequently will go around the house, peering into the windows to see me. They'll wait by the front door when they think I'll be coming out to feed the horses. Often they scare people who come here. They're not used to seeing a raccoon stroll down a barn aisle at 12 o'clock noon. My farrier nearly fainted the first time he saw this, as he frantically pointed at the raccoon walking toward us. There are also two red-tail hawks that have a nest up in a tree next to the house. They'll usually be riding the air currents above the horse pasture, but occasionally they alight on the fence and just hang out there to watch what's going on. I feel quite honored that they chose me as their friend.

Callie Mae, the Cat with No Legs

Of course I love all of them, but some animals stand out, ones that I will never forget, whatever the reason. Maybe they have a big personality, a terrible life before I rescued them, or they are handicapped in some way. I actually seek out handicapped animals to adopt, because I know no one else will want them, and they'll end up getting abused or killed. The cat that totally stole my heart is Callie Mae, a cat with no legs that I saw on a news program from Mobile, Alabama. I was walking through the room just as the segment came on, the newscaster saying they were looking for just the right person to adopt a cat that had lost all her legs after being electrocuted. As I write, Callie Mae's right next to me, curled up in her soft bed, keeping me company.

Callie Mae's former owners used to let her outside. When she was just six months old, a pack of dogs chased her up a telephone pole. When the owners called to her to come down, Callie Mae stepped on the power line, got electrocuted, and fell thirty feet to the ground. They rushed her to a vet and told the vet to do whatever it took to save Callie's life. The cat stayed in a coma for three days, and was in such bad shape, the vet didn't think she was going to make it. One of her front legs was shattered so badly, it had to be removed. Over subsequent days, after Callie Mae came out of her coma, her other three legs showed signs of disaster from being electrocuted. The flesh was infected and festering. Over the next six months and through multiple operations, Callie Mae gradually lost all four legs, a little bit at a time.

All of this surgery and care took its toll both financially and emotionally on the owners. Finally, they told the vet they just couldn't do it any longer. The vet kept

Callie Mae for the next two years. She already had a five-year-old son, and then had another baby. Between working as a vet and the two children, it was too much for her. She decided to go on a quest to find Callie Mae a special person, who could take care of this cat with special needs.

The instant I saw Callie Mae on the news show, I knew I had to have her. It was love at first sight. I immediately contacted the vet and left a message, then repeated it the next morning. As fate would have it, the next day at work I saw Linda, an operating room nurse I'd known my many years. Linda knew I loved animals and rescued them, and had given me a tiny kitten several years earlier. I knew Linda lived over in Alabama, near where that vet was located. I asked her if she'd seen that news segment about the cat with no legs, and she replied, "That's my vet." I nearly fainted. I told her I desperately wanted Callie Mae, because I knew I was the right person for her. Linda got out her cell phone and called the vet's office. The vet wasn't available, but the technician who took the call had known Linda for a long time. Linda told her about me and that I wanted the cat. The woman passed that information on to the vet.

Two days later the vet called me, and we talked at length. That was a Monday night. That following Sunday, the vet drove over an hour to bring Callie Mae to my home. Of course, the cat took to me like a duck to water. Callie Mae is the star here, and gets pampered like a little princess.

Because she doesn't have any legs—well, she actually has about two inches of each leg—she can't use a litter box like other cats do. Instead, she goes on a towel. I got Callie Mae a big playpen, and she's got her bed in there, along with an elevated feeding and water bowl area. Over the rest of the area, I laid down a thick foam cushion, a plush rug on top of that, absorbent pads, and then a towel on top of the pads. I wanted everything extremely soft for her little legs, so that when she climbs out of her bed, she's comfortable. She loves to watch TV with my mom, and I hold her often, giving her many kisses and hugs. She loves when I rub her ears and tickle her belly. She spends a lot of time purring. Callie Mae is lucky that I got her, but I'm even luckier to have her in my life.

Callie Mae, my little sweetheart

My Big Dream of Starting a Sanctuary for Rescues

One thing I cannot do, is see an ad on TV for an organization like the Humane Society of the United States, where they start showing homeless cats and dogs, and not burst out crying. Or some animal show in which something terrible happens to animals. If I'm at work and happen to see that on TV, I quickly get out of the area so I don't see the show and no one else sees the tears flowing down my face. I always dream of winning the lottery, so I can get a one-thousand acre facility to start a sanctuary. I would take in hundreds of animals, cats, dogs, horses, all farm animals, and have employees to help me take care of them and hug and pet each and every one every day. The animals would live out their lives in comfort and love.

The Person in the Horse Suit

Lars was my most beloved horse. He died five years ago, and I'm still not over it. He was a spectacular horse, standing a majestic 18.1 hands tall and weighing over 2,400 pounds. He was half Thoroughbred and half Clydesdale, and had all the markings of the Budweiser Clydesdales—dark brown body, four white stockings up to his knees, the big white blaze down his face, and black mane and tail. I always said he had a Thoroughbred brain in a Clydesdale body, and for those who are familiar with hot-blooded Thoroughbreds, that's a scary thought! The biggest thing about Lars—or Larzie, as he was affectionately known—was his overwhelming personality. He was a real

Larzie, my most beloved horse

people horse, or as I'd call it, a busybody! If he was in his stall, his head would always be over his gate as he looked at everything going on. He didn't want to miss a trick.

When I'd have him on the crossties to brush him and get him tacked up, he still had to keep track of my every move. When he wanted a treat, he'd hold up a front leg like a dog would do. When you talked to him, he would shake his head up and down as if he knew what you were saying. When I was on his back, I was sitting on top of the world. It was as close to heaven as I could get. Of all the horses I've ever ridden in my lifetime, and they probably number in the hundreds, not one of them had a canter like his. It was like riding a giant rocking chair. Of course, it wasn't always like that.

The Snowflake Ride

There are moments in one's life that are remembered forever. The Snowflake Ride was one of those times for me. I was living in Wisconsin, and it was the first day of April. I was riding Larzie in my outdoor arena. A herd of deer had just run down the hill behind the barn. It was always a treat to see those majestic animals, and I would get an adrenaline rush whenever I was lucky enough to see them so close. Larzie heard them before I saw them, and he spun around to get a look.

I had just asked Larzie to canter, and he had settled into his spectacular collected canter when it started to snow. This wasn't unusual for April in Wisconsin, although it seemed a bit warm for it that particular day. But there they came, big flakes falling gently, like in slow motion. I was sitting deep in the saddle, leaning my weight back, giving Larzie the signal to sit deeper on his haunches and go even slower. He was so collected, cantering so slowly, with all those huge silver-dollar snowflakes coming down around us. I was totally mesmerized, and then I started laughing in delight. I didn't want that moment to ever end. We kept going, that rocking-chair canter, snowflakes swirling around us. I put my head back to feel the flakes hitting my face. When we finally did stop, I leaned forward and threw my arms around Larzie's neck, and thanked him for one of the greatest moments of my life. He shook his head up and down like he was agreeing with me! The snowflakes were landing on his eyelashes. I sat there on that powerful back for quite some time, just savoring the experience.

The Horse I Just Had to Get

When I purchased Larzie, he was not quite four years old, but was already going under saddle. I first watched him on a videotape after seeing an ad in the *Chronicle of the Horse* about a a Gifted look-alike. Gifted was a Grand Prix dressage horse that had been in the past two Olympic Games, and he was my idol. I got to see him in person once at Gladstone, the United States Equestrian Team's Olympic Training Center. I can still remember my awe at the sight of that spectacular horse. He was 17.3 hands, dark brown with four white stockings up to his knees, a white blaze down his face, and a black mane and tail. Breathtaking. A real showstopper. So, when I read about a a Gifted look-alike for sale, I was calling faster than you can blink an eye! The videotape of the horse arrived a few days later. I hurried to pop it into my VCR. Well, there he was, and yes, he looked just like Gifted. I wanted this horse. Of course, normal people try out many horses before they actually buy one, but I didn't care about anything except I *must* have this horse!

The owner kept insisting that I come up to Minnesota to try him out. I was living in Cross Plains at the time, just outside of Madison, Wisconsin. I couldn't be gone from home for that long to go that far away, so I asked the owner if she'd trailer him down. I'd pay her to do so. The next weekend she arrived at the boarding stable just around the corner from me. I'll always remember when she opened the back door of her trailer, and there stood the most humongous horse I'd ever seen. He backed out and started looking around, snorting. It was snowing. He had a thick winter coat. She led him into the barn, and he was still snorting. We went to take him into the indoor arena. When I opened the big sliding door, he looked up at the ceiling, and then literally buckled his knees and went down on the ground. His owner laughed, saying he'd never seen an indoor arena. By now I was a bit scared of him. I'd never seen any horse react to something new like that.

After we got him up, she walked him around for a while. He got quite scared when he saw the glass windows of the lounge. I was getting more nervous by the minute. I wasn't looking forward to being on top of something so huge that also seemed to be scared of everything. We finally went back into the barn and put him on crossties. At that time, his name was Gibraltar. Yes, like the rock of Gibraltar. She called him Wally for short.

That wasn't going to remain his name, I thought. We brushed him and then tacked him up. She was going to ride him first. When we took him back to the indoor arena, he didn't collapse. She got on and rode him for about seven minutes, and then it was my turn. As I led him over to the mounting block, I started hyperventilating. I swung my leg over his wide back and settled into the saddle, and I suddenly felt like I was on top of the world.

I no sooner picked up the reins than he took off at a full gallop. Several other people were riding in the arena, and they quickly got out of our way. I brought him into smaller and smaller circles, until finally I was able to stop him. His owner had been watching in horror. She came rushing and said, "Oh, you shouldn't have had your spurs on." She reached up to take them off my boots. I had on my blunt tip spurs, which were a necessity when riding warmbloods, which is what I'd been riding for the past several years. Warmbloods, for nonhorse people, are huge European breeds that tend to be lazy and need some encouragement to get them working.

I was quite scared to try riding again, but I did. I realized I was going to have to do a lot of figuring out to ride this horse. If you tried pulling on the reins he only went faster, and the faster he went the more unbalanced he became. I'd need to make him rebalance his 2,400 pound body. What a challenge, I thought, and of course I bought him. I renamed him Lars Leksell, after a famous neurosurgeon.

Riding Larzie's incredible collected canter

Obsessed with Dressage

I started riding dressage when I was twenty-nine, just after I graduated from Columbia University and passed my anesthetist board exam. A horse friend from my younger days was into it, and she kept her horse at a big riding center in New Jersey, not far from New York City. She called me to tell me about a horse for sale that she thought would be a great schoolmaster for someone just starting dressage. I made an appointment and went to try the horse, which was being sold by an Olympic rider. This horse was twelve years old and had been trained for the highest level of dressage. That was exactly what I wanted, a horse that could teach me what all the movements of dressage felt like. It was evening when I arrived at the barn, and they had the horse on the crossties. Inside the barn were pendant lights, which made this horse look like he was made of patent leather. He was jet black except for a tiny snip of white on his nose. The one thing I will always remember was seeing his tail literally hanging down along the ground. I mentioned that, and owner said, "Wait until you see him go, and you'll see why we don't cut it." The horse was 17.1 hands and was a purebred Trakehner, a German breed.

The owner took him into the indoor arena. After warming him up, she started showing off all the dressage movements he was trained to do. She then hollered, "Okay, everybody, watch this!" With that, she came around the short side of the arena and started across the diagonal in an extended trot that knocked my eyes out. The horse was literally floating across the arena. It was beyond spectacular, and everyone was gasping. Now it was my turn. I was so excited. Once aboard, it was a dream to ride him. He was so responsive to my every command, and any shift in my weight was a signal to him to do something. I was not used to such luxury. Also, I was just starting in dressage and wasn't really familiar with how to do it. Even though I was an experienced rider, riding jumpers was a whole different ballgame from dressage. Riding this horse, whose registered name was Adler, was like magic. I didn't want to get off, and I rode for quite some time. I renamed him Teimuraz, or Timmy for short. I got the name from a Russian dancer who was with a dance troupe called the

Georgian State Dance Company. The troupe was from Tbilisi, Georgia, which was under Soviet rule at that time.

Teimuraz grazing in Wisconsin

I had met this dancer while I was a student at Columbia. His dance company was performing at Lincoln Center, and he injured his knee, tearing ligaments in the joint. They brought him to the hospital where I was doing my training, and I did his anesthesia for his surgery. The next day when I went to see him post-op, he started flirting with me, and we talked for some time. His English was good enough, so we could communicate fairly well. He was discharged from the hospital a few days after his surgery, but his troupe was going to be in New York for another two weeks. We continued to see each other for that time. I got to go backstage at one of their shows to meet all the other dancers and see behind the scenes. It was an exciting experience. So, I thought the name Teimuraz was just great, and that's how I named my very first horse.

I kept Timmy at that riding center and trained with the Olympic rider—whom I'll call Susan—for the next two years. She taught me all about dressage, and I learned how to ride all the movements of it, all the way through Grand Prix level. This trainer was always training quite a number of privately owned horses, and she often had me ride those horses for my lessons. Her reasoning was that it was best to experience lots of different horses and be able to ride them all. I loved it, because these were all expensive horses and well-trained horses. I recall one horse in particular, who was named Mirando and was about fifty hands high—or seemed like it, anyway. He was as long as a freight train and simply massive. Susan wanted me to ride this horse to learn passage, a highly animated trot that looks as if the horse is suspended in air. She said he had a great passage, but it was difficult to put him together to do it. Only a very experienced rider with very strong legs and seat could even attempt it. After warming him up, doing some exercises to stretch him down and then bring him into collection, Susan said it was time to work on passage. I was the only one in the indoor arena riding, but a small audience had gathered.

I was riding Mirando at a collected walk along the long side of the arena, and Susan was walking alongside me. "Okay, Anita," she said. "Just think passage."

I looked down at her from my towering perch. "What do you mean?"

She leaned back with her upper body to demonstrate. "Just sit deep, squeeze tight with your legs, and imagine he's passaging."

Well, by gosh, I did exactly what she said, and suddenly I was nearly lurched out of the saddle! Mirando had started passaging, and the thrust of it was so surprising. It took me a moment to get into the rhythm and follow it with my back and seat. I then kept him in it, and we passaged most of the way around the arena. Everyone started clapping and cheering. What an exciting moment! I remember Susan saying that no one could get that horse so collected and on the bit like I could.

Over the following years I learned all I could about dressage, and treasured every ride on Timmy, who was my best teacher. I knew how to train a horse to do dressage, because I now knew how to do it correctly. One of my highlights was taking Timmy for dressage clinics at the United States Equestrian Team Olympic Training Center in Gladstone, New Jersey. The facility is nothing less than spectacular, from the one hundred acres or so that the facility is on, to the stable area with white hand-laid bricks, to the huge 12' x 12' stalls with dark oak planks and solid brass bars and trappings. I would have been happy to live there in a stall, it was so beautiful! I watched Olympic riders training there, and videotaped them. At home, I'd study the footage to figure out what they were doing, so I could try to emulate their skills. Seeing Olympic horses was exciting, too, horses you'd see in all the big-time horse magazines. It was truly an honor to be there, and I cherished each and every time I went. I remembered every minute too. All those experiences laid the foundation of my dressage skills, which I would later need when I got Larzie. Boy, would I need them, each and every one of them!

Teaching a Massive Horse to Balance Himself

So now I was the proud owner of Larzie, the massive Thoroughbred Clydesdale cross that I was scared to ride! I started out riding him at the walk, getting him on the bit and really up in his back. After mastering that, we proceeded at the trot, which went well. The canter wasn't so good. Each time he got unbalanced and started to run away. Back to the trot and walk. That literally went on for months. I found a trainer, Kate, who was an upper-level dressage rider, who had spent several years in intense training in Europe with dressage masters there. When she rode Larzie, she'd get him balanced and have him cantering around in a slow, collected canter. I'd watch in disbelief. Why couldn't I figure out what to do with him? Kate tried to explain to me what she was doing, and it did get a little better for me. But it wasn't until several years later, when I hooked up with a dressage trainer named Sandy, that it all fell into place.

I met her in the middle of winter; she arrived at my place for our first lesson just after a big snowstorm. The snow was deep, and it was a bit slippery underneath. I had built a barn and a big outdoor arena on my land, and kept Larzie at home. I figured we would mostly walk with all the snow. After explaining to Sandy the ongoing problem with Lars at the canter and him getting unbalanced, she explained that he started going faster to sort of catch up with himself.

After I had just walked Lars for a while, with Sandy talking to me, she said, "Now you are going to canter."

I looked over at her like she was nuts. "On this slippery ice and snow? I'm going to get killed when he starts running away."

"Well," Sandy replied, "Lars is real smart, and *he's* not going to want to fall down either. Just sit really deep, brace your back really stiff, hold your outside rein tight, and *shove* your inside leg into his side."

Taking a deep breath, I did all of the above, after asking Lars to canter. Instead of careening away, Lars sat back on his haunches and went into a huge, rocking-chair canter, just like the one he'd do when Kate rode him. I couldn't believe what was happening. We kept going all around the whole arena. I didn't breathe until I brought him back to a walk. Stopping, I literally burst out crying tears of joy. I'd done it! I had finally done all the right things to make it work. When Sandy said I had to *shove* my inside leg into him, that's exactly what I had to do, with all my might. In dressage, the concept of inside leg pushing into outside rein is not new, and I did it on every other dressage horse I rode. But with Lars, probably because of his massive size, the pushing with my inside leg had to be as extreme as his size! The interesting thing, though, he was very sensitive in his mouth, like a Thoroughbred usually is.

From then on there was no stopping me. Over the coming years, I trained Larzie to do all the dressage movements that I had learned on all those wonderful horses. I trained him by myself, and I had him so well trained, anyone could ride him, even a young child. Each and every ride was a gift. I'm very grateful to have owned him, but after he died, he took a part of my heart with him. I don't think I'll ever love a horse like I loved Larzie.

He died at the age of sixteen from colic. Despite thousands of dollars and the vet's multiple attempts to save him, he died right in front of me, in his stall. Moments before he died, he suddenly perked up and nodded his head yes, like he frequently did. His eyes seemed interested, and I had a fleeting thought he was going to make it. Then he reared up and crashed to the floor, thrashing, his eyes rolling, looking like he was having a seizure. I stared in disbelief. He was dead. My most beloved horse, my dear friend, the person in a horse suit, the one who always made me laugh and the one who gave me the best rides in the world. To say I became hysterical is an understatement. My memory after that is a blur, and I think my mind blocked it out, because I really don't like to think about that moment. It's bad enough when a person loses their dog or cat, but losing a horse that gave you his all, on every single ride, is beyond devastating. In my dressage magazines, when I open a page and see a photo of some beautiful horse with the headline, "In loving memory," I quickly turn the page. Still, I cry as I think of all my wonderful times with that incredible horse that I'll never forget.

Riding across Snow-Covered Fields

Another riding highlight was on Timmy, when he was twenty, riding him bareback in the snow. I was living in Wisconsin then, and I had him at a boarding stable. It had snowed about two feet the day before, but now the sun was out in its full glory, and the air was cold but dry. Timmy was already retired and hadn't been ridden for months, but that day I decided to venture out into the snow. After brushing him, I thought, *why bother with the saddle?* So I put on his bridle and took him outside by my truck, which I used as the mounting block. Once aboard, I decided to simply head out across the corn field and enjoy the countryside. The snow looked like it had millions of diamonds glittering across it, and all the trees were laden with snow, their branches bending from the weight of it. Without a saddle, I could feel all of Timmy's muscles moving under me, and I was enjoying watching his face as he looked around. I let him wander where he wanted to. The sky was so blue and so clear, the air so crisp, I had a wonderful feeling of being one with the universe. I'm not sure how long we walked, never leaving sight of the barn, but up and down the gentle, rolling hills. Timmy had been my dressage schoolmaster, who had taught me everything I knew, but that ride—our freedom ride as I sometimes call it—is the one I remember the most.

All My Cats

As I write tonight, Thomas the Monster Cat is right next to my laptop, snoring in his fluffy pink bed. He earned the title of Monster Cat because of the destructive things he does. He's a huge sixteen-pound Maine Coon cat that I adopted from a shelter in Alabama when he was four. He's now nine going on two. He'll jump up on a table and walk all around it, shoving everything that's on it onto the floor, and watching excitedly as the objects crash to the ground. I'll be in another room and hear glass breaking, and I'll remember that dish I should have taken into the kitchen and which is now shattered all over the floor. I have to constantly try to remember not to leave stuff on the tables or counters. It's actually quite amusing to watch him shove things overboard, because he'll take an item that's in the middle of the table and slowly push it toward the edge. When he gets there, he then sits down for the final push.

I am a germ freak, and I'm constantly scolding Thomas for jumping up on the table or counter. That never seems to work, but when he sees me reaching for the spray bottle of disinfectant to clean the area he was just on, he runs mighty fast to get away from me.

In the morning when I'm putting my makeup on, Thomas jumps up on the sink and "hugs" me. He stands up on his hind legs, reaches up with his front paws, wide apart, and hugs me, while looking up at me like I'm the greatest thing since sliced bread.

Thomas the monster cat

Whitey

One of my most beloved cats was Whitey, a pathetic little cat I adopted when she was sixteen, by default. I had adopted a Himalayan cat I named Miss Himmy, and when the lady brought Miss Himmy to my house, she just happened to bring along Whitey. She stated that Whitey and Miss Himmy were best friends, and, "Oh, by the way, Whitey is stone deaf." She was pure white, an albino, with light blue eyes. She also was blind in one eye and had a bad heart. Of course, I took her too. She lasted four more years, but ended up getting cancer. Whitey didn't want to go, and up until her very last day she followed me all around the house. She was so weak, she barely could stand. I got brave enough and called the vet, who came to my house to peacefully do the dreaded deed. I sat in a chair with my little sweetheart in my arms, sobbing, as I am right now, as she went off to her final sleep. The one bad thing about writing this book is reliving those terrible moments. I keep trying to remind myself of all the years of happiness she brought me, and how happy I made her as well.

Whitey by her stuffed animals, age 20

Climbing out a Window with a Kitten Hidden in My Clothes

One of my first cats was Panny, short for Pancake. At the stable where I worked as a teenager, stray cats were forever showing up. Stray probably isn't the right word. Abandoned is more accurate. The woman who managed the stable, the Purple &

Orange Witch, had a young daughter who would take a shine to some of these cats. She'd take them into the lounge on the far side of the indoor arena, with the intention of feeding them and keeping them. Her intention may have been good, but more often than not, she'd forget to tend to them and they would die. It happened regularly.

One day, when I was fifteen, a new kitty appeared, a tiny, meek light gray kitten. She was in the lounge, which is where the office was, several soda and candy machines, as well as chairs where people sat to watch riders in the arena. This lounge was different from the one across the arena, because this one was for the public. The other one was bare, and only the Purple & Orange Witch and her two daughters had the key for it. This frail creature was scared of the other cats in the lounge. When someone put food out for them, she'd attempt to eat, but then the other cats came barging over. She'd flatten herself like a pancake and slip under the candy machine.

I heard that Terry, the P&OW's younger daughter, was saying she has her eye on this kitten, and was going to take it over to the other lounge. I called that lounge the temple of doom, because that's what it was for most of the cats she took there. So later that day, when my mom came to pick me up, I went into the lounge, made sure no one was looking, picked up Pancake and put her under my shirt, and then went into the ladies room. A window in there faced the street, and I had told my mom that I needed her to park directly in front of that window. There was only one big problem, as I discovered when I looked out the window. Directly below the window was a well that dropped down about ten feet. Getting out that window took some skill, but I did it without killing myself or dropping Pancake. I had tucked my shirt deeply into my pants and placed her inside the "pocket" I'd made. I climbed out the window with extreme caution, holding on to the sill and getting my feet on the metal rim that surrounded the well. In the process of this great escape, someone came walking up the sidewalk to the front door of the building, just a short distance from me. He looked suspiciously over his glasses at me, and I just smiled. He never said a word.

Once at home, I made Pancake very comfortable. Over the following weeks, Terry and her mother put up signs all over the barn asking if anyone had seen the tiny gray kitten, and if they did, please bring it to them. I returned home and asked Panny if she wanted to give up her soft kitty bed, the best of wet and dry food, and lots of love, for the temple of doom. Panny said no, and I had to respect her request. Thus, Panny lived with me for the next nineteen years.

It was sort of ironic what happened about two months after Panny died. I was shopping at the Short Hills Mall in Short Hills, New Jersey, and who was walking toward me but the Purple & Orange Witch. I was very tempted, very tempted indeed, to go up to her and tell her that I'd taken that little gray kitty her miserable daughter had been looking for. I had spared the cat a death of starvation and dehydration, and instead gave her nineteen wonderful years. I didn't speak to her, just looked her right in the eye as I passed her. To this day, I'm sorry I didn't tell her. I'll have to remember to send her a copy of this book when I get it published, with this page marked. And guess what colors she was wearing at the mall? Yup. Purple and orange, and she looked more like a witch than ever.

Although I've already discussed the Purple & Orange Witch, there's more to offer on the subject. Years after I had left that stable, she purchased a horse facility out in the country, about an hour from the barn. I read an article about her and what happened at her place in a horse magazine, and the article made me very suspicious. The author of the article seemed suspicious too. A mysterious fire destroyed her stable, killing a dozen horses and the two people who lived above the barn. They were supposed to have been gone for the weekend, but they'd gone only a few miles when their car broke down. They walked back to the barn and went to bed, and there they died in the fire. The article stated that the Purple & Orange Witch had not been able to sleep, and at 3 a.m. happened to go for a walk around the grounds. She even noticed that the husband and wife who lived above the barn were gone, because their car was not there. Some time later, that building burned to the ground, killing the horses and the couple.

Chickens Make Great Pets

I've always loved chickens, and a year ago decided it was time to build a nice facility for some. That turned into a five thousand dollar venture! It ended up being a huge complex, with a nice house with all their nesting boxes, gangplanks, and a long run for them. After it was built, I wanted it totally secure with metal cloth, as it's called, a strong mesh fencing that would protect them from the raccoons and hawks that are so common around my house. I'm sure the carpenters were just thrilled about this, as they had to crawl around on their knees to deal with the bottom part, and then get up on a ladder to cover the top and sides of the run and the ceiling inside the house.

Meanwhile, I had gone to my local feed store with a bunny cage to put my new chicks in. In the feed area, there were racks and racks of week-old chicks of several varieties, but inside the store was a bunny hutch with a few chicks in it. I decided I wanted the ones in the hutch, so the worker went over to open the lid. The chicks immediately clustered together, though it looked like there were about four, maybe five chicks. He asked which ones I wanted, to which I replied, "All of them." While he was putting them in my cage, I walked away to get the chick feeder and watering device. He brought my cage up to the register, which was where I discovered that I was purchasing eleven chicks! *Oh, well,* I thought. *What's the difference?*

They were only a week old, and they were so tiny that as I was driving home with the cage on the passenger's seat, some of them were popping out between the bars of the cage and walking around on the seat! I realized this about halfway home, and had quite the time keeping my eyes on the road. Once home, I had to cautiously open my door to get out without anyone escaping, and then went to get a cat carrier to transport them to the barn.

I kept them in the tack room from September until April, because it was a lot warmer in there. I also kept a small battery-powered lantern in their cage at night so they wouldn't be scared. They would gather around it like it was a little powwow. They were the most precious little things when they were wee ones. It was fun watching them grow up into adult chickens. I started picking them up from the first day I brought them home, so they would think of me as their mom. And they do, to this day. When I go outside by their condo, they all come-a running to me and follow me all around. Some of them clamor to get picked up. Their eggs are delicious, probably because they get the highest quality feed and sunshine. When I watch all their silly antics, like taking dirt baths, I feel sorry for chickens raised commercially for slaughter. Those chickens live in squalor, jammed together by the millions. They never experience the joy of wandering around out in the sunshine, free range, just having fun. My little chicks will live out their lives in luxury, with lots of love as well.

Thanksgiving Day Massacre

I have dreaded writing this part of this chapter. I'm still suffering from the events of that day. They have left an indelible image in my mind that I'll never be able to cleanse.

I have three dogs, two Great Pyrenees, about one hundred and fifty pounds each, and a ten-pound Maltese. They have my sunroom and a huge fenced area that's about half an acre, with an eight-foot fence, as their world. They love to spend most of their day outside, digging holes, soaking up sunshine, barking at hawks and raccoons.

On the Wednesday before Thanksgiving, I was at work for fourteen hours. I normally call home several times throughout the day to check up on my mom. She said everything was fine with her, but she was concerned about the dogs outside. She said they were barking and barking, nonstop, most of the day. She wasn't able to go to the door to check on them, but insisted something was unusual in their behavior. When I got home that night, they were quiet. I thought perhaps the raccoons were more active than normal.

After changing into my comfortable clothes, I got to work in the kitchen preparing stuffing and cranberry sauce. My mom and I chatted away as I diced and sautéed all the ingredients for the stuffing; and while that was baking in the oven, I put together the cranberries, sugar, and water in a pot and put it on the stove. The popping sound of the cranberries always amused me. It was nearing midnight when the dogs started barking wildly.

"See, see," my mom said. "That's what they were doing all day."

Yes, it was different from their usual barking. I'm not a fan of going out in the dark to investigate things, but I did step out the back door to see if I could determine where the dogs were looking. They were all lined up looking toward the cottage, where the eighteen cats that I have rescued over the years live. Then, just like that, the dogs stopped barking. I stood there for a while, and then returned inside. That was the last time they barked that night. I was having such fun doing all the cooking, little did I know the horror that was happening to some of my beloved cats just one hundred feet away.

Several years earlier, a builder had purchased a fifty-acre parcel of land just across the street from me, which had a big lake in the middle of it. His company started preparing the land to put fifty homes back in there. Within about a week of this activity, stray cats began appearing around my house. Eighteen of them to be exact. I began trapping them in a have-a-heart trap and taking them in batches of five or six to my vet for spaying and neutering. On my property is a 1,200-square foot cottage that I used for storing stuff. I cleared out half of it and had a carpenter enclose the front patio with heavy lattice, so that the cats would be able to sit out on the patio, get sunshine, but still be enclosed and safe. That patio work cost over $4,000. I had special "hospital" cages that I kept the cats in for a week or two after their surgery, depending if they were male or female, prior to allowing them into the whole area. There was a fireplace in there, and I had a rocking chair by it so I could sit with the cats. Several of them remained feral, but over time most of them came over to me and let me pet them, eventually climbing up onto my lap and sitting there. I would have cats piled up all over me, and it was just great. I'd pet them and talk to them. It was a wonderful time to relax and recharge my batteries. These cats were part of my daily life, and I loved each and every one of them.

Thanksgiving morning arrived, and I was up early to get the rest of the big dinner prepared. I was planning for us to eat at noon. It was about eight when my dogs started up with the wild barking. I looked out the huge kitchen window that faces the courtyard between my house and the little cottage. In the instant before I got to the window, I realized there were more than my own dogs barking out there. Sure enough, when I looked out, I saw two dogs trotting around, looking like they were having fun, barking every now and then. One was black, and the other one, the smaller one, was red. What I did notice immediately was that they were extremely skinny. I could see all of their ribs and each vertebra down their spines. Right then, they trotted past my window toward the front of the house. Being the soft-hearted person that I am for animals, I felt sorry for these pathetically skinny dogs. I put on my shoes and grabbed some cans of dog food, intending to go out and feed them. I couldn't stand the thought of a hungry animal, least of all on Thanksgiving. It took me several minutes to finally get outside. I didn't see the dogs anywhere. I walked around the side of the house, but no dogs in sight. Since I was already out there, I decided to go and feed the cats in the cottage. *Might as well get it done now,* I thought, *before I get into all the cooking.*

I opened the outer door of the cottage, which opened into a vestibule. Fishing out my keys, I opened the inner door and stepped inside the house, into the storage side, as I called it. One third of the main room was partitioned off with fine mesh fencing to keep the cats out of the storage side. I added a screen to access the cat side. From the storage side, I could see everything in the cat side, including the doorway that led out to the lattice-enclosed patio. At that time of the morning, the sun would be shining from the patio into the big room.

I closed the inner door behind me and looked into the cat room. It was truly incomprehensible to my brain what I was seeing, though it took only a moment to register it all. There, just on the other side of the screen door, directly in the sunbeam shining through the doorway, were those two dogs, standing side by side, growling a very deep growl at me. The next image that hit me, the image I'll never forget, was the sight of dead cats strewn all over the place, their bodies ripped to shreds. I then spotted the huge gaping hole out on the patio in the lattice, a hole the dogs had ripped open to get in there. I became hysterical in that moment. I then did something so stupid, I still can't believe I did it. I turned around and ran out back to my house. I had my cell phone on me, so why I didn't just call the police from inside the safety of the storage area, I don't know. Once inside my house, I called 911. A deputy was there within several minutes. I started telling him what happened, and he said he saw the two dogs heading down my back driveway just as he was arriving. He wanted to follow them. He left, and about forty-five minutes later an animal control officer arrived. I was sitting, in a state of shock, inside my front door. I didn't know where those dogs were. Just before the animal control officer arrived, the deputy called me to inform me that he had followed the dogs for two miles, right to their home. He went to the house to inform the owner of what their dogs had done, and that animal control would be coming to take them away. The deputy also told me that both dogs were pit bulls, and the owner had other pit bulls chained up in his backyard.

I desperately wanted to go back into the cottage, but really couldn't risk it. I didn't know if any more dogs were loose. When the animal control officer arrived, he wanted to hear the story. Then he wanted to go see the crime scene. When I walked into the room and looked at my beloved cats that were dead, I was sick beyond words. They had been family members. One of the cats, Mario, was a big tabby cat about seventeen pounds. His fur used to be so shiny, and there he was, all stretched out dead, his fur matted with dried saliva and blood. Another one, Fabrizio, was literally torn open from one end to the other, with his intestines pulled out all over the floor. I thought I was going to faint. There were six dead in all. When we walked out onto the patio, what I saw had my heart leaping for joy—six cats were clinging to the beams up in the ceiling. Their eyes were bugging out of their heads. Those poor little things. What they had witnessed, and the fear they must have felt, was horrendous. I cried with happiness to see them, but then I realized there were six unaccounted for. I'll never know if the dogs killed them, too, and took them through the gaping hole in the lattice, or if they escaped during the massacre.

As I'm writing tonight, it's been four months since Thanksgiving. Every time I go into the cottage, I still envision those two dogs standing in there in the sunbeam. I was issued papers from the county, stating that both dogs had been euthanized. I felt relieved not to have to worry about them ever returning. I did feel bad when I looked at those papers, and I also thought that the owner of the dogs should have been punished more than just being fined. Besides the fact that he allowed them to roam the streets, they were emaciated and starving.

The Singers

I love birds, all kinds of birds, so I have a variety of seeds in the bird feeders outside my house. It is peaceful and relaxing to simply sit with a cup of tea and watch them eat. My new Asperger's friend, Marilou, also loves birds and is quite the photographer. At her home, she created a blind to sit in, so she can photograph all the birds coming to the feeders. She then e-mails me the beautiful photos, with a tag saying what kind of bird it is. I've been learning many new birds since we've become friends. It might sound silly to some, but I could just sit and watch all those beautiful birds for hours. I love to listen to them singing, and to hear all their different songs.

As you can see, I love animals. Besides their beauty, I love the inner peace they give me. When I'm with an animal, whether it is a cat, horse, or dog, I always look into their eyes, into their soul. It makes my soul feel good. It also makes me happy to make my animals happy, by giving them a loving home. I wish I could help more animals. I wish I could have that big sanctuary someday for rescues, the ones who need us most.

My friend, Marilou Lehmann, sent me this great photo she took and included this message: "This little tufted titmouse reminds me of you, because he goes for the gusto and comes out on top, nothing too big to conquer!"

Chapter 9:

Hurricane Ivan: Making It through a Category 4 Hurricane

I was at work and walked into the lounge during a break. Everyone in there was talking, reading the newspaper, and joking around. No one besides me was paying attention to the weather report on the TV. They were showing a hurricane that was gaining in size and strength, and its path could mean a direct hit on Pensacola, Florida. Beads of sweat started pouring down the center of my back. I looked around the room, but still no one else was looking at what was becoming a monster hurricane. I said out loud for people to listen up. No one paid attention to me. I walked out of the lounge feeling very, very nervous. True, the weather people wouldn't be able to pinpoint the path for days. I was hoping it would wander in some other direction.

It didn't. A few days later, I was scurrying around, getting everything in place in preparation for a hurricane, like putting shutters on the windows, securing everything outside, things like that. It was early on a Wednesday morning, September 15, 2004 to be exact and the hurricane was due to make landfall in less than twenty hours. We made the decision not to stay at the house during the storm, because of all the huge trees around it. I had made reservations at a hotel on the west side of Pensacola, in an area I felt would be safe. I had also requested to have a room at the east end of the hotel, close to the parking lot. I was going to be smuggling several cat carriers into the hotel's back door, right by our room, after dark. I wasn't about to leave my precious cats at the house. I didn't have any dogs yet, nor any chickens. I got all of them several years after Ivan.

After checking into the hotel, we tried to relax in our room. I was waiting for darkness to start the smuggling process. I had parked my truck right outside the window so I could check on the cats. Every so often I'd go out and sit in the truck to be sure they were okay. They were each in a carrier, and I'd given each one food and water. In the room we watched the live coverage of the approaching storm, appropriately named Hurricane Ivan, like Ivan the Terrible. We would soon find out just how terrible it would be. I later learned that Ivan was the tenth most intense Atlantic hurricane ever recorded.

I walked across the street to get some food from a nearby burger place. It was packed and I had to wait forty-five minutes. While I was there, they announced they were closing in two hours so their workers could go home. On my way back, I stopped to admire a huge pine tree that stood in front of the hotel on a nicely manicured island. It had to be the biggest pine tree I'd ever seen. It was magnificent.

By the time we finished eating, it was dark enough to bring in the carriers, one by one. I was hoping no one would see me, and hoped the cats wouldn't decide to start meowing. I feared we'd get thrown out of the hotel if they suspected I had cats in the room. Finally all six carriers were in the room. I fed the cats, and they went to sleep. We did likewise.

Around eleven thirty, I got up and turned the news back on. Suddenly the power went out, as expected. I got out my battery-operated lanterns, which made creepy shadows on the walls. The cats started getting restless. You could hear the wind picking up outside. The one thing I had forgotten was a radio. Now we wouldn't hear any news of what was happening.

The wind was really getting strong. You could just sense it pushing against the walls of our room. I realized that the east end of the building probably wasn't the best location. Just outside the building, against the east wall of our room, was the fire escape stairwell. Our room was on the ground floor. I had already moved all the carriers into the bathroom, so they were away from the windows. Mom and I were sitting on chairs that I had moved in there as well. Abruptly, things seemed to change. The wind became deafening, and we got into the bathtub. The pressure on our ears made them pop. Then there was a massive sound, yes, like a freight train, right outside the building, which was beginning to rock back and forth. It felt like we were in a vacuum, and it seemed to last forever. You could feel and hear massive damage happening to the building. We just closed our eyes and waited to die.

Then as quickly as that, it all ended. The fire alarms in the building started going off. In that instant I imagined the building was on fire, and that we'd be standing outside in a category 4 hurricane. Someone pounded on our door, and a man yelled that the outer stairwell has been ripped off along with the whole top floor of the building. He was screaming for everyone to get into the main foyer of the hotel. By now my Asperger's nerves were totally frayed. I felt like bursting out crying, but there wasn't time. We had to get out of the room. But I wasn't going to leave the cats in our room. When we made our way down the lantern-illuminated hallway, so came all the carriers. As we walked down that hall, doors from all the other rooms were opening, and out came all the occupants. Much to my shock, more animals came as well. Cats in carriers, parrots, dogs, including a huge Great Dane. There were bunnies in cages, and ferrets. As everyone gathered in the lobby in silence, we all just looked at each other and all the animals. It was surreal. No one said a word. Not one animal made a peep. All we heard was the wind howling at over 130 mph.

Water poured down wherever there was a light fixture or any opening in the ceiling. Now that the roof was gone from the floor above us, the rain was just filling up the rooms upstairs, finding its way anywhere it could. The water was ankle deep. The light fixtures from the dome in the foyer started swaying, and as I looked up, I could see the walls moving. Here came that overwhelming feeling of doom. The stress was stupendous, like nothing a person could ever imagine. I ran back to our room to get stuff to put the carriers on, to keep them out of the water.

About two hundred people were standing against the walls. We were all just waiting. Waiting to die or waiting for the storm to ease up. It was now about two thirty in the morning. Someone had a small radio with the news on. They had just announced that the eye of the hurricane had shifted to the west, going right into the mouth of Mobile Bay. It was starting to ease up for us. Everyone simultaneously raised their arms and started cheering. I was beyond exhausted by this point.

By 5 a.m. the wind finally eased up. I was waiting for daybreak to go outside and look around. Reports were starting to come in on the radio of catastrophic damage to the area, including some deaths. I was terrified by now. Finally, it was light enough to go outside. To this day I still remember the shock at what I saw. It looked like a war zone. The entire top floor of the hotel lay in the parking lot. The air was filled with the smell of freshly cut pine trees. I looked over toward that beautiful pine tree I had admired less than twenty-four hours earlier. It was snapped in half, with the jagged trunk sticking up. I slowly walked over to the tree and stared at it in total disbelief. The force of the wind had snapped the massive tree in half. I turned around and saw others filtering out of the hotel, looking at the destruction that was everywhere you turned. Everyone was silent. We were all walking around like zombies. That's what I felt like. My mind really couldn't absorb it. A few walls remained of the hotel, but the rest of it was strewn all over the parking lot. Several cars had been crushed by concrete slabs.

I walked around the side of the building by our room. My eyes got even bigger. The fire escape was in ruins, torn totally off the building. Also torn off were most of the bricks and siding of the wall that made up our room. We had been literally feet from the wrath of the tornado that devoured the building. It gave me chills just looking at it, and I wondered what would have happened if the walls had been totally destroyed, like the roof. I tried not to think about it. We had learned during the night that tornadoes are extremely common during hurricanes.

Thankfully, my truck was safe. We checked out of the hotel and loaded the cats in their carriers into the backseat. The ride home normally would take about ten minutes. This time it took almost two hours. Trees down everywhere, road blocks, power lines dangling from utility poles snapped in half. What a sight. Finally we arrived at our road. Huge trees lay across it, so we turned around and tried getting access from the other side. That was even worse. Going back to the original side, we parked the truck as close as we could to the back driveway and set out on foot.

I made my way down the road to the front of my property by climbing over the downed trees. When I arrived at my front driveway, I looked down toward my house, and then stared in shock. Dozens of huge trees were down all over the house and driveway. It looked like the house was totally gone. I will never forget that sight. I hollered out to my mom that the house was destroyed. I couldn't get to the house from the front; and by now I was also getting hysterical, worrying about the horses I had left out in their pasture. That's what I had read to do with horses during a hurricane. Just leave them out in a pasture, and they will know how to take care of themselves. Never, ever lock them up in a barn.

As fast as I could, I made my back out to the street and down to my back driveway. The smell of pine wafted through the air. I finally got to the back of the house, where I could see the huge sixty-foot trees that had crashed into it. I was straining my eyes to see down to the pasture. I couldn't see any horses. Considering the catastrophic destruction all around me, I was trying to prepare myself for the horses' deaths. It seemed impossible that any animal could have survived. The high chain-link fence around the backyard area was nearly inaccessible. I couldn't open the gate because there was a tree down across it. I was getting more frantic by the minute, trying to get the gate open. All I wanted to do was get to the pasture to see if the horses had made it. Suddenly, the gate sprang open, and I ran through it, racing toward the barn. I still didn't see any horses. Then I heard a horse neighing loudly. At that moment I saw Larzie and the other horses standing down in the ravine, and when they saw me, they all galloped up toward the fence. There are no words to describe my relief and joy at seeing them. I fell to the ground, sobbing with happiness. Everything was hitting me like a ton of bricks. All the stress and terror I had just gone through simply overwhelmed me.

I looked toward the barn and gasped in shock. It looked like a massive explosion had taken it down. One wall was left standing, the front wall of one of the stalls. The halters still hung neatly on their hooks. I could see the path of the tornado, which had obviously touched down, from its well-defined swath of destruction. I was beyond thankful that I had read the article about never putting horses in their stalls. They all would have been dead had I locked them up in that barn.

We were able to stay in one end of our house. Nothing is more surprising than opening a door to a room in your house and seeing several huge trees in there, and the sky where there used to be a roof.

The next wave of stress was about to begin, and it would last an entire year as the house was rebuilt. The horse barn was finished by the end of December, but it took a full year to rebuild the house.

The power was not restored for eight days. I spent the first few days walking the neighborhood to find people to get the trees out of my house. Wherever I heard chainsaws or bulldozers, I walked in that direction. The phone service didn't get restored until December 28. That was three and a half months without phone service.

During the whole following year, there was an endless stream of workers in and out of the house. All the trusses had to be replaced on one end of the house, and the roof rebuilt. All the carpeting had to be removed, as well as any furniture that had gotten wet when the trees came through the roof. For someone with Asperger's syndrome, that year was just never-ending stress. I honestly don't know how I made it through the whole process.

One thing I clearly remember is those eight days when the power was out. Each night the sky was crystal clear, and the stars looked like you could reach up and grab them. It looked that way because of total darkness everywhere, which made the stars brighter. I really felt like we were cut off from the rest of the world. Very isolated. For an Aspie, that was extremely overwhelming, but there was so much for me to do, I really didn't have time to be upset.

Chapter 10:

Famous People Who Have Influenced My Life

There are a number of famous people who have greatly influenced my life, in one way or another.

Oprah Winfrey

Recently, Oprah Winfrey said something that was so profound to me, I started to cry. She was talking about her best friend, Gayle King. Oprah said it was incredible having Gayle in her life, since she is her best friend and like a sister, and it was wonderful to have her friendship. I cried because I've never had any friendships, let alone such an obviously wonderful one as Oprah and Gayle have. At that moment, I realized I needed to write this book, to allow others into the world of a person with Asperger's syndrome. Normal people rarely give having friends a second thought. They just have them, and it's a normal way of life. For an Aspie, you are always on the outside looking in.

Meeting Oprah is one of my biggest dreams, because I want to educate the world about what Asperger's syndrome is really like. I've seen shows that try to depict someone with Asperger's, and it's usually very disheartening to me, because the portrayals are grossly distorted or embarrassing. I want a platform to get the word out, paving the way for others who have Asperger's syndrome. I especially want to help the children, who struggle in their classrooms because the teachers and administrators don't know what it is or how to deal with students who have it. I want to be an advocate for Asperger's syndrome, to help the millions of people with it. I want to emphasize to them that even though you have fewer circuits in your brain for social skills, that leaves you with more pathways for talents and skills. I started a support group for Asperger's syndrome, and I can see in our small group of twenty-five regulars, both children and adults, the need for the public to get educated about Asperger's; and the need for parents to take a "tough love" approach to their AS children. This is my new special interest, one that I'm going to pursue with my heart and soul.

Scott Hamilton

I greatly admire Scott Hamilton, and think he's a tremendous inspiration. Despite all his health issues, he maintains the positive attitude that helped him win Olympic gold in men's figure skating. No skater could ever match his spectacular footwork, which he always did at the speed of sound.

Yanni

The next famous person who's a big part of my life is Yanni. Whenever I write, I play his album, *Love Songs*, very softly. I can't write without that playing. Several years ago Yanni had a concert here in Pensacola that I was lucky enough to get to see. I sat right in the front row, and it was an overwhelming experience. I later read his autobiography. Now that I know all about Asperger's syndrome, I can't help but wonder if Yanni has at least some Asperger traits, such as his ability to focus intently when writing his beautiful, complex music. He wrote in his book that when he is on a roll, he'll stay holed up in his recording studio for weeks at a time, sleeping in there and having family bring him food and leave it outside the door. He wouldn't talk to anyone during this time, in order to maintain his focus. Very Asperger. I wish I could meet him someday.

Tom Cruise

Tom Cruise is next on my list, for starring in *Top Gun*. It was that movie, which I watched in 1995, that kicked my Asperger's special interest into high gear and urged me to pack up and move from Wisconsin to Pensacola, Florida, to be by the Blue Angels, the Naval Air Station Pensacola, and Eglin Air Force Base. His inspiring character, Maverick, sent me into a tailspin and set everything in motion. After seeing that movie, I wanted to fly in a fighter jet, and that's all there was to it. Somehow, some way, I was determined to pull off this stunt. I had absolutely no idea how, but I had the determination to do it. I spent the next seven years working toward that goal, which I finally obtained on December 6, 2002, when I got a flight in an F-15 Eagle. This whole story is told in the chapter, *Top Gun* Changed My Life.

Lady Gaga

Lady Gaga is another person who inspires me, especially after I saw her being interviewed by Larry King. She talked about being bullied when she was young, and not fitting in. I admire her incredible creativity, and actually consider her a genius in what she does. I've lost track of how many times I've watched the video for "Bad Romance." It's probably higher than the US debt! Her latest song, "Born This Way," is my new theme song.

Susan Boyle

Susan Boyle inspires me to just keep going and believe in myself. It took a lot of courage for her to walk out on that stage and sing. I'm thankful she did, and I hope it taught a lot of people to stop judging someone on first impressions. Susan's voice is so beautiful, so rich. She, too, was bullied. I hope everyone who bullied her feels like an idiot now.

Anderson Cooper

Anderson Cooper could be living off his family's wealth, but instead he chooses to be a top news reporter, among the best in the world. He travels the globe to be where the action is, and all too often, where the danger is as well. I had admired him for years before I found out who his mom was. One day I was reading something in a magazine about Gloria Vanderbilt, and she made reference to her son, Anderson Cooper. I nearly fell off my chair. Both my mom and I have admired Gloria for years, and have been using her perfumes and accessories forever.

Anderson's coverage of Hurricane Katrina was incredible. He lived right there in New Orleans for weeks after the storm. I'm always terrified that Pensacola is going to be hit by another bad hurricane like Ivan in September 2004. The one consolation would be that Anderson Cooper would show up here and I might get to meet him! There were rumors flying during Ivan that Anderson was in downtown Pensacola at a pub called New York Nick's. I've never confirmed that story. I really wish I could meet Anderson someday, as I know I could talk to him for hours.

Temple Grandin

Temple Grandin is the world's most famous person with high-functioning autism. She has a PhD in animal science and is a professor at Colorado State University. She is also a best-selling author, a consultant to the livestock industry on animal behavior, and a leader in both animal welfare and autism advocacy. She travels around the world to give speeches on autism, and has dignified and improved the lives of millions of people with autism.

When I watched the movie about Temple's life, I cried at many points. Asperger's syndrome is on the autism spectrum, and most everything Temple experienced, I experienced as well. The scenes of her being laughed at by her classmates brought back all my memories of school days. The scenes of her getting fixated on some small detail and people's reactions to her ... Yes, I've been there. I also think in pictures, as she does, and was actually shocked to learn that other people don't also think like that. I always assumed everyone thinks that way.

I'm impressed that Temple pursued her dreams, which became reality. Many others would have given up when faced with such adversity.

I hope to follow in Temple's footsteps and do for Asperger's syndrome what she has done for autism. She gives hope to parents of children with autism and adults with autism, that they can overcome obstacles and rise to the top.

Dr. Tony Attwood

Dr. Tony Attwood is the world's leading expert on Asperger's syndrome, with over thirty years of experience with individuals with autism, Asperger's syndrome, and pervasive developmental disorder (PDD). He is a clinical psychologist from Brisbane, Australia. Dr. Attwood has worked with several thousand people with Asperger's, and his books and videos on Asperger's syndrome and high-functioning autism are recognized as the best in the field.

Dr. Attwood's book, *The Complete Guide to Asperger's Syndrome,* was the first book I read the night I discovered I have Asperger's. I can still remember the state of shock I was in as I read every word, because it was as if he had known me from the day I was born, and understood exactly how my brain worked. Anyone with Asperger's syndrome must have that book.

James Durbin

I'm so proud of James Durbin for performing on *American Idol,* showing the world the talent of someone with Asperger's syndrome. James performs like a professional singer, and his stage presence is awesome! I'm rooting for him to be the last one standing on that stage on the final night of voting. He is an excellent example of what having Asperger's syndrome can do for you, when you direct that laser focus on something you love to do.

Chapter 11:

Past Relationships

I've had three romantic relationships in my life, though none in the past fourteen years. Looking back, it is obvious that the ones I had were determined by my Asperger's syndrome. If I were to meet those same guys today, there would not be a second date. There probably would not even be a first date, because I wouldn't be interested in them at all.

At this point in my life, I know exactly what I would want in a man. Unless I find that, I'm quite happy to be by myself. It is probably difficult for normal people to understand that I am extremely happy being alone. There are so many things I love to do, solitary things, and I don't need someone else to make them happen. Another factor in finding a man to have a relationship with, he would have to be able to accept someone with AS. Despite the quirks that go along with Asperger's, I have a lot of great stuff going for me. One thing is for sure: I've never had the dream of getting married, a big wedding and all that. In fact, I look at the bride's magazines on the racks in stores in disbelief, that this is such a big thing to normal people. I've heard women over and over talking about their "big day" as the most important event of their life. I've actually known women who booked a big reception hall for a date several years in advance for their wedding, even though they didn't have a boyfriend. They were sure they'd find one to marry by then.

I love to be home. It is my castle. I love to cook and bake; in fact, I'm quite the gourmet chef. Because AS people are detail oriented, anyone who gets a dinner is treated to a delicious, eye-appealing culinary delight. I consider the plating and presentation as important as the food itself. I love being around my animals, and get a real kick starting out my day by going out and gathering eggs from my hens, and then coming in and cooking up a nice country breakfast.

I love reading about forensic stuff. Years ago, when I worked at a big hospital up north, I had a high-profile prisoner as my patient. I had to talk to him in the pre-op area, and it was fascinating to look at this soft-spoken man, talking so calmly and pleasantly, while knowing what he had done to so many people. From that I got interested in researching the criminal mind, and started reading books by John Douglas, the FBI's most famous criminal profiler. I can't explain my fascination with the criminal mind, but in light of all the TV shows about this genre, a lot of folks have the same interest.

I love to be in the woods. My idea of a great time would be a week in a log cabin among trees, where I could enjoy nature with long walks. I would probably do some writing, because I'm inspired by nature.

A recent interest I've developed is shooting my gun. I enjoy going to the rifle range and seeing how well I hit the targets. When I was a kid, I loved to go to the fair and shoot the fake guns at the gaming area, as I'd always win a stuffed animal for my "sharp-shooting" skill. Even though I wear my ear protectors, the sound of each shot does go through my whole body, but the fun overrides the sound aspect. It is a real adrenaline rush. I used to do archery when I was younger, and was quite good at that too. I would like to get back to shooting arrows again. All this shooting is only at targets. I would never hunt, for the obvious reason of my love for animals. I cringe when the hunters I know at work talk about their success over the weekend. Paper targets suit me just fine.

I love to write. I've already written a romance novel and will pursue getting that published next. Upon completion of this book, I'll immediately start another one.

I also love to talk to someone who's intelligent and a good conversationalist. As a matter of fact, that is the thing that would most attract me to a man—that he's smart and can carry on an intelligent conversation.

I'm totally honest and sincere. I'm not into mind games. One, because they don't interest me; and two, because it is literally impossible for an Aspie to know how to do that. I wouldn't have a clue how to manipulate people. The wires never got connected!

My first boyfriend was an engineer, who was thirty-five. I was eighteen. Looking back, I can see why my mom was less than thrilled with this relationship. My first trips away from home were with him. He loved to ski, and four times he took me to Canada, to a place called Mont Sutton, a ski resort sixty miles east of Montreal. It was extremely beautiful there. The relationship, however, was very shallow, the sort an eighteen-year-old with AS would readily fall into. I was extremely naive and didn't see the forest for the trees. It lasted three years.

The Deep Dark Secret

My next venture was a guy I met at a formal ball that my mother dragged me to. This fellow, whom I'll call Richard, was the guest of honor at the affair, along with his mother, Mary. He was tall, extremely handsome, very romantic, and lived to go to formal affairs. I had to learn the Viennese waltz to participate at these events. I still had some issues with coordination, and learning this particular style of waltz was no small feat. It involves a lot of spinning and turning as you go. I quickly got dizzy and almost sick whenever Richard tried to teach me. He would get annoyed that I wasn't learning it as fast as he thought I should. Eventually I could do it, but not for very long, because the dizziness would creep up on me.

Our relationship revolved around shallow things like attending formal affairs and being around lots of people. This was a constant struggle for me, but I tried to keep that hidden. Our romantic encounters were movielike, which was the best part of the relationship.

Things changed during the fourth year of the relationship. Richard would often take me to his grandparents' farm, just outside Princeton, New Jersey. The farmhouse was over one hundred years old. It sat on twenty acres, and it was extremely peaceful there. Yet for some reason, I had a strange feeling whenever I visited. I couldn't explain it; it was just there. Then one day I discovered that my feelings had a real reason to be present.

Richard always wanted to go to this club in town that he and his whole family belonged to, as well as their friends and extended relatives. They were all German and Austrian, and this was what the club was about. Each time we went, Richard would go hang out with the other men, and I'd sit with his mom and the other ladies of the club. The ladies were all elegant, and the conversations revolved around planning teas, luncheons, formal affairs, and such fine festivities. I always wondered what the men discussed.

One night I found out. I excused myself from the ladies to go to the powder room. Just around the corner was the big heavy door to the room where the men met. I cautiously walked over to the door, trying not to make the old wooden floor creak. Ever so slowly, I pulled the door open just a bit—and got an eyeful. Richard and all his buddies were watching a black and white film of Hitler, and they were lifting their arms in the Nazi salute, chanting "Sieg Heil" over and over. My hair stood on end. I didn't like the looks of this. Just as I started to pull the door shut, Richard turned and saw me. I quickly exited the building and went outside for some fresh air. He was right on my heels. At first he was angry that I had ignored his instructions never go into that room. Then he calmed down, saying that the next day, he wanted to share something with me.

That night, lying in bed in that old farmhouse, I started getting the creeps. What was he going to show me the next day? I finally drifted off to sleep.

Morning arrived quickly. At breakfast, his mother and grandparents announced they would be gone most of the day to visit relatives. As soon as they left, Richard took me upstairs to a spare bedroom. He had me sit on the bed while he opened the closet and took out a huge box. Placing it on the bed, he unlocked the box and lifted the lid. Inside were some very strange items. There were swastika armbands, all sorts of medals, and a black military uniform. The hat that went with the uniform had a distinct symbol on it—a skull. A belt had an insignia that read *Unsere Ehre heisst Treue*, along with the double s symbol of the SS. I didn't want to touch any of these items, though he kept trying to hand them to me. It all looked like death to me.

The worst part came, when he proudly told me his grandfather had been in Hitler's SS, the Shutzstaffel, which were originally Hitler's personal guard unit. There also was a copy of Hitler's *Mein Kampf*, which means my struggle.

Richard placed all the items back in the box and, holding my hand, led me down the hall until we were standing in front of a heavy wood door. He told me that this door, along with two others in the house, was hollow and filled with gold ingots from melted gold fillings and jewelry. An image instantly flashed into my mind of the thousands of dead bodies all that gold had come from. Inside I was literally hysterical. I wanted out of that house. Then I realized that the instinctive feeling I always had there was from these things. I don't believe in ghosts, but I think the spirits from all those souls were probably present in that house.

Somehow I lost that loving feeling toward Richard that day. We had quite a huge fight, and then it was over. He was a Hitler and Nazi sympathizer, and believed Hitler was the greatest man who had ever lived. Up until that day, there had never been any hint of this; and it took me years to recover from being involved with someone whose grandfather was in the SS, and who revered the Nazis.

I don't know if his mother ever knew why we broke up, but for some reason I contacted her a year or so ago. She had always been very nice to me. We've talked on the phone several times since then, but one call in particular I remember well. It would make for a great Stephen King novel. Mary called me on Halloween night and told me she had just returned from the farmhouse. Mary now lived in her own apartment. The grandparents had been dead for a few years, and her brother had recently died too. They had all been cremated, and their ashes were in urns in the farmhouse. Mary had had the electricity shut off because she no longer lived there, but she would regularly go check on everything. She said a terrible thunderstorm was raging, and when she went into the farmhouse, the lightning was striking all around the farm, the thunder crashing. It also happened to be Halloween night. She mentioned checking on the three urns with the ashes of her brother and parents, the SS grandfather included, and my thoughts raced to the three doors filled with the gold stolen from thousands of Jews that had been brutally murdered in the Holocaust. The image of all this would make quite the movie scene.

The Brain Surgeon

It was some years later that I had my next romantic adventure. I was working at a nice hospital in Bucks County, Pennsylvania. A neurosurgeon had just started working there. My first encounter with him was less than pleasant, but pretty funny. It was a Saturday, and I was on a twenty-four hour in-house call. Nothing was going on in the operating room, but I wandered out of my call room to get something from my mailbox. The lights of the OR were turned off; the only light was in our little anesthesia office. I walked in and was taken by surprise by a man standing there wearing street clothes, not scrubs. I asked what he was doing there.

"I'm looking for coffee," he said.

"Well," I stated, "there isn't any here. And further, you're not supposed to be here in street clothes. Who are you anyway?"

"I'm the new neurosurgeon," he said, and he turned and walked out.

What a jerk, I thought.

The following week I ended up working with the new surgeon a number of times. The first day was a bit uncomfortable, due to our rocky first encounter. After that, our relationship started blossoming. I eventually learned, though, the dark secret that haunted him his entire life. He had a serious problem with sex. He was great at kissing and cuddling, but he would get very tense and strange beyond that. He would usually cry afterward. One day I saw a talk show about men who had been sexually abused when they were a child. When they mentioned the signs to look for, he was it. The poster child for being sexually abused as a child. That night I told him what I'd seen on TV. He started crying and blurted out that it had happened when he was an altar boy. The priest had abused him, and it went on for a number of years. He told me not to ever bring the subject up again, because it was too painful for him to think about. I never said another word about it. We were together about three years, but it was a strange relationship. He felt most comfortable talking about neurosurgery.

I have often wondered how I found these unusual men, and if they were drawn to me because I was different. Like I said earlier, if I met these same men now, there wouldn't be a relationship. The older I get, the more I know exactly what would attract me to someone. Looking back, now that I know I have Asperger's syndrome, I realize just how much that played a part in each of those relationships.

Chapter 12:

Being Estranged from My Brother

I've read in a few Asperger books that it's not uncommon for a neurotypical sibling to dislike his or her AS sibling, and to shun them, as is done by peers out in the world. I experienced this firsthand with my brother. I wish things were not like this, because it would have been great to have another family member besides my mother as a friend and support person.

My brother is nine years older than I, and for reasons too lengthy to explain here, we were not raised together. We did have time together growing up. One thing he had that I didn't have was lots of friends. His peers were the most important thing in the world to him. He was raised by our grandparents, and when he turned sixteen they gave him a new Volkswagen Beetle as a birthday present. He was off and running with that car, using it frequently to tote around all his friends, sometimes eight at a time stuffed into that small Beetle. He also used it to enter road rallies, a regular weekend event. When he started college, he and a bunch of his friends rented a house to live in, so they could have loud parties and lots of friends coming over at all times. This house was in the same town as my grandparents', as was the college he was attending. He got married during his last year in college.

Contrast this to my life at that time: no friends, living home with my parents, and not wanting to learn to drive because it was too overwhelming to me. The only place I went, besides school, was the riding center, and my mother drove me there. This really bugged my brother.

One night, when I was eighteen and he was twenty-seven, something happened that forever changed our lives. He was married already, and he and his wife were at our house, as were two of the neighbor's daughters, Jenny and Leah. We were all sitting around the dining room table eating, when for some reason, my brother started in on me about not having any friends and not having a boyfriend; and that I hadn't gone to the prom, and I didn't drive. The others joined forces with him, calling me names and saying all kinds of horrible things about me being so abnormal. Mom finally was able to break up the argument. The two neighbor girls went home, and everyone went to bed. Still, the atmosphere was tense.

My brother couldn't get over his fixation, and first thing in the morning he started up all over again. Finally Mom solved the whole thing. She ordered him and his wife out of the house and told them not to come back. They packed up their bags and out they went, the last we'd see of them for the next ten years.

Mom's mother was dying. Grandma was eighty-six years old. On her deathbed, she begged my mom to repair relations with my brother. Reluctantly, Mom and I did start talking to him again, but it was very strained. We talked now and then over the years, but it was always a struggle. It would be easier to talk to a complete stranger.

He visited us when we lived in Wisconsin, and he brought the woman he was dating at the time. He had been divorced several years already. Then he met someone else and got married again about seven years ago. He and his wife have been to my home in Pensacola several times with their two young children.

The last time they were here was about a year ago. Mom brought up the topic that I have Asperger's syndrome. This made him very angry, and he walked outside to avoid talking about it. He knows very well what it is, because he has a PhD in psychology, and is a dean and professor at a large university. He couldn't pretend he didn't know what Asperger's syndrome is. Regardless, it still made him very angry. I had a pathetic hope in the back of my mind that once he knew this, he would have some remorse over what he did all those years ago, all those horrible things he yelled at me, and apologize to me. Keep dreaming. Actually, his reaction only made me feel more estranged from him. I just sigh and accept it. I have tried. I did not succeed, but at least I can say I tried.

Chapter 14:

Unable to Tolerate Loud Music
and Certain Visual Effects

Sensitivity to noise is often the biggest challenge for people with AS to cope with. What neurotypical people think of as normal places, such as grocery stores, concerts, restaurants, parties, workplaces, and sporting events, can be a nightmare to an AS individual. Typically, the AS person avoids these places, except obviously the workplace.

Every AS person I've talked to, and those I've read about, avoid going out. There are restaurants I know to never step foot into, because the music will be blasting. If I walk into a new restaurant and the music is too loud, I'll turn right around and walk out. Grocery stores are notorious for playing loud music, and it always seems to be something harsh and annoying.

I am aware of some people with AS that enjoy loud music, but that's a minority. Often those people will play musical instruments, and they play in a band, or sing. In their cases, they can use their acute hearing to their musical advantage.

Noise in the workplace can also be challenging, from the sounds of machinery in operation to the sounds of people talking. Obviously, this cannot be controlled, so people with AS need to find ways to cope with their particular situation.

I have an unusual situation in my work environment. As an anesthetist, I work in operating rooms all the time, with different surgeons and different operating room staff. Many surgeons don't like any music playing while they operate, while several of them want to turn their operating room into a concert hall. These particular surgeons will bring either CD players or their iPods, complete with speakers, and set them up on a cart in the room. One in particular loves heavy metal, angry music, and will turn up the volume to the max, so that anyone in the room has to go over to the person they want to communicate with and yell to them in order to be heard. The sound can be so loud that the surface of my anesthesia machine, where I keep the chart that I write on throughout the case, is vibrating from the noise. I once watched my pen vibrate all the way off the machine. Obviously, I cannot work in this environment. I sent a request to my boss, asking that I not work in this surgeon's room. Although my boss knows I have AS, his response was that my letter was a "direct attack" on the surgeon, and that he needed to listen to his music in order to function. This floored me. What an answer. Additionally, I wonder if any of his patients' family members would think it's okay to have music like that.

Other surgeons who like loud music and know I have AS are gracious, and they turn the volume low to accommodate my hearing sensitivity. I am most grateful to them.

I can listen to certain music without any problems, but things with high, harsh, grating sounds make me physically ill. Before I learned about Asperger's, I'd be puzzled by my physical reaction to certain kinds of music. Now I know why I'm reacting to it the way I do. People have said to me, when I complain about the music, that it's all in my head. They are correct. Only, I was born this way and can't help it.

Visual Effects That Bother Me

Years ago a few things happened to me from visual effects, but I didn't know why they happened. Now I do.

The Pier

On Pensacola Beach is a pier that juts 1471 feet into the Gulf of Mexico. I went out to the farthest end one day shortly after it opened. The weather was spectacular, and the Gulf was its usual incredible emerald-green and turquoise. The sun was out in its full glory, creating sparkling diamonds on the surface of the water. I was mesmerized by the beauty of the water and stared down at it for quite some time. I was searching for exciting things, like a few stingrays that kept lazily gliding around the pillars of the pier, and an occasional dolphin.

When I returned home, all I kept seeing in my mind was that sparkling water and the motion of it as waves rolling in toward the shoreline. I became so ill, so dizzy, just sick all over, that I had to lie perfectly still in bed for the next fourteen hours. No matter what I did, I could not get that image out of my head. Needless to say, I never went out on that pier again.

I've come to learn that type of problem is common to people with AS.

Nutcracker Suite

When I was living in New York City, while attending Columbia University, my mom and I were regulars at Lincoln Center. On one of our visits, we saw the *Nutcracker Suite*. I was enjoying myself very much, until the mice sword fight stared, and strobe lights flashed. As I watched the strobe lights on the dark stage, I started feeling very, very strange, like I was going to pass out. I quickly told my mom how I felt. She later said that when she looked at me, my eyes were rolling back in my head, and I looked like I was going to faint. I think if I had watched that stage one more minute, I would have.

I've learned that people with AS react like that to strobe lights. So now I know to quickly look away from any type of flashing lights.

I like indirect lighting, and even candlelight. I like to make a fire in the fireplace, pull up my favorite chair, light the lantern, and work on my book. It is like an old-fashioned feeling, and it is very relaxing to me.

The other AS issue is visual thinking. Between that and my hearing sensitivity, it's like living in perpetual surround sound and high definition! When I'm thinking, I see a huge movie screen in my mind. I always just assumed everyone thinks like that.

Extreme Sensitivity to Touch

As is typical with people on the autism spectrum, people with Asperger's syndrome are extremely sensitive to certain fabrics and types of clothing. As I mentioned earlier, I cannot stand to wear socks. I cannot wear any fabrics that are scratchy, stiff, or rough. I remember childhood dresses made of stiff, scratchy fabrics. It was not a pretty picture whenever I was trapped inside one of these torture chambers.

The people who know me or see me regularly can easily recognize me from my "uniform": soft black cotton slacks and a black, soft peach-skin button-down shirt.

My Extreme Sense of Smell

My sense of smell, like my other senses, is greatly heightened. This is terrific in the spring when my wisteria is blooming. I'm in my glory then. On the other hand, while at work, it is the exact opposite. Certain types of cases have extremely unpleasant odors. When working on those cases, I have to put two or three masks to try to fend off the smell. The problem with all the masks is, I'm nearly suffocating. If a case lasts four hours, I'll feel like I'm on the verge of fainting the whole time. In addition to near-suffocation, everyone in the room is laughing at me because I have on all the masks. I've explained over and over that when you have Asperger's syndrome, your sense of smell is like a dog's. To me, that horrible smell that everyone else smells is one hundred times worse.

Chapter 15:

Advice for Parents of Children with Asperger's Syndrome, Educators, and Adults with Asperger's Syndrome

Although there are many books available for parents of children with Asperger's syndrome, most of them are written by psychologists. Not to undermine the knowledge of psychologists, but there is nothing that can compare to the experience of someone who actually has Asperger's syndrome and has lived it with it her whole life. Especially in my case, where I didn't find out what Asperger's syndrome was until I was forty-nine years old. It was sort of like seeing the movie first and then reading the book!

My whole life I had been plagued with an endless list of obstacles to overcome, or at least try to overcome, and I thought they were unique to me. After learning about Asperger's, I was both amused and saddened to see that all the things that affect me, also affect everyone with Asperger's to one degree or another.

From the support group that I started several months ago, I can see the vast differences in people on the Asperger's spectrum. Just as everyone is a unique individual, so are their Asperger's traits. This is what makes it so difficult for neurotypical people to deal with us. Most people I know have no idea what Asperger's syndrome is; or, if they say they do and I ask them to state it, what they say is incorrect. One woman I know has a young child with AS, and she said that she's not worried about it. Her pediatrician told her the child will outgrow it around age twelve. So there's a doctor who doesn't even know what AS is all about.

Center for Autism and Related Disabilities

Here in Pensacola, Florida, is a local CARD chapter, which stands for the Center for Autism and Related Disabilities. It was established by Florida State University in July 1993, and is one of seven CARD centers funded by the Florida legislature. There are offices in Tallahassee, Panama City, and Pensacola. I am very lucky that there is one here in Pensacola. CARD serves individuals of any age with autism spectrum disorders, including autism, Asperger's syndrome, Pervasive Development Disorder-Not Otherwise Specified, Rett syndrome, and childhood disintegrative disorder. Related disabilities include the deaf and blind, and hearing- or vision-impaired with other disabling conditions. CARD also serves family members, friends, and professionals associated with CARD clients.

CARD provides direct services to eligible individuals for communication, social, and behavior problems, and provides information, consultation, and technical assistance to families and professionals. In addition, the center offers training and partnerships to professionals and preprofessionals who serve, or are preparing to serve, the client population.

The Americans with Disabilities Act

The Americans with Disabilities Act is something that every parent of an Asperger's child *must* learn about, as well as every individual with AS, to fully understand how you are protected by this law. It protects against bullying, harassment, retaliation, job termination, and more. It is very serious if an employer or school violates this act, because it is federal law.

Power Point

Become familiar with the Americans with Disabilities Act at <u>www.ada.gov</u>.

Your Child with Asperger's Syndrome in the School System

When I was in elementary school, the teachers and principal had no idea what to do with me. One day I was placed in a class of mentally-handicapped children. Had my mother not been the tireless advocate for me that she was (and still is!), who knows what would have become of me. From all the people I've met with Asperger's, mine apparently was not an isolated case. Even though my experience was back in the 60s, this type of thing is still happening to children in schools today. I keep hearing over and over from the parents of Asperger's children how they are constantly called to the school about some disruptive thing the child did, or the parents have to go in to complain about something that was done to their child.

Despite the fact that it's now 2011, teachers and school administrators don't seem to have a clue about Asperger's and how to deal with it. Below is an example of that. Amanda is in my support group, and shared this story of an event that happened recently to her at school.

Amanda is a sixteen-year-old high school student. One day, the noise level in class was getting out of control. All the other students were talking and horsing around, creating chaos. Amanda had reached her saturation point of sensory overload. She picked up a desk and dropped it, creating a very loud thud, and stated, "This place sucks!" Everyone did shut up at that point. But instead of the teacher realizing that the students had been out of control, and that Amanda couldn't cope any longer with all the noise, the teacher called Amanda's mother to the school to discuss her behavior.

If the teacher had really known what Asperger's syndrome was, and that having heightened sensory awareness was part of it, she would have realized that Amanda wasn't the bad guy. She was the victim.

I hear these types of stories over and over, from parents with children in elementary school through high school. *Something needs to change.* And that's my job, to start changing it. All teachers and administrators need to be thoroughly educated about Asperger's syndrome, and understand the needs of people with it.

Power Point

Educators and parents need to be able to differentiate bad behavior from sensory overload. Don't treat them the same. AS children cannot help their reaction to stimulus overload.

Why Employers Need to be Educated about Asperger's Syndrome

Employers need to become educated about Asperger's syndrome, not only for on the job, but for the interview process as well. Following is an example of why this is necessary.

A man who has a twenty-one-year-old son with AS works for a well-known delivery service, delivering packages to residences and businesses. He took his son with him for several months to train him to do the job, which involves scanning each item at each stop, logging it into the data base, and then dropping off the package. The son quickly learned the whole process and was enjoying the job, so his father arranged an interview for his son to apply for the job. Having Asperger's syndrome, the young man feels uncomfortable meeting new people in a new environment.

Consequently, he is not at his best in interviews. He did go for the interview, but he did not get hired for the job, even though he already knew how to do it very well.

Had the interviewer known about Asperger's syndrome and known that the young man had it, the process might have gone differently and he might have been offered the job. Although the young man lacks social skills, the company would have a reliable employee who would do a great job for years to come.

Also, employers need to learn about AS to help them understand that for an AS employee, their behavior is normal to that individual. I once had a boss tell me that he couldn't figure out if I was for real or if I was pulling his leg. I'm always "for real." What I say is how I think. That's how my brain is wired. To me it is normal.

Power Point

Try alternative methods of getting a job, ways that would enable you to let the boss know you can do the job, and do it well, despite the fact that you are not a social butterfly. Perhaps do some volunteer work in the area you are interested in to get your foot in the door. Utilize parents, teachers, and neighbors who might have a connection to the prospective employer to help you out. Don't be afraid to ask for help.

Also, once employed, help your employer become familiar with AS and its characteristics. An AS person can change to some degree, but will still function according to how he is wired. If problems in your workplace are not being resolved, be aware that you can seek out assistance by contacting the EEOC, the federal agency for the Equal Employment Opportunity Commission.

Helping Your Child Find Something He Loves to Do

One thing I try to emphasize to parents of children with AS is that they should do everything they can to help their child find something they love to do. Hopefully they will be able to turn that into the job they'll do for life. By being exposed to many experiences, sooner or later they'll find that special interest that will set off the Asperger's laser focus, with the drive to pursue this interest to the fullest degree. Don't overload the child by signing him up for endless lessons in a multitude of things. Take your time. The child needs some peace and quiet.

Something that annoys me is parents who think that because their AS child loves playing computer games, they are going to be the next computer guru. Building and programming computers has little to do with playing video games. In other words, don't let your kid spend six hours a day playing games on your computer. Use time wisely.

Neatly Groomed for the Workplace

Having AS is associated with inconsistent personal hygiene. I'll be the first one to admit that I'll leave the house to go grocery shopping, or even to work, with my hair uncombed and in wrinkled clothing. I use the excuse with work that I arrive to the hospital at 5:30 a.m. and who the heck sees me then. I go to the operating room locker room and change into "pajamas," otherwise known as scrubs. (As I mentioned earlier, I wear scrubs that are two sizes too big, so I'm not irritated by the fabric.)

At my support group, a sixteen-year-old boy, talking about his "wild-looking" hair, said that if it was okay for Albert Einstein to have hair like that, it's okay for him to do it too. I agree!

The reality is that you do need to look good on the job—clean, neat, hair combed, teeth brushed. For an interview, select an outfit that's appropriate, probably subdued and conservative. You are trying to get a job, not show off your taste in clothing. And guys, try to wear socks for the interview. I admit that I don't wear socks, because I can't stand the feel of them on my feet. Once in a while I'll try to wear them, and by the time I'm walking to my vehicle, I've got to stop and take the socks off. But for a job interview, just try to suffer through it.

Be an Advocate for Your Child

For parents of AS children, your biggest job is to be their advocate, not only out in the world, but in the home. Self-esteem, or the lack of it, is an obvious problem that AS children (and adults) struggle with. Starting in elementary school, children with AS will normally be the last ones picked for a team, they'll be bullied by their peers, and they'll always present issues for their teachers to deal with. There will be obstacles to clear every step of the way, even once the AS individual is an adult and out in the work force.

Maintaining Your Positive Thinking Even When Bad Things Happen

I was watching a talk show this morning and Scott Hamilton, Olympic gold medalist in men's figure skating, was one of the guests. At one point he said, "It's not about falling, it's about getting up." He was referring to the obstacles in life that everyone faces, and how you have to get yourself up after falling. For people with AS, there are a lot more obstacles to overcome in our everyday lives; and though that is sad, it is true.

From the earliest that I can remember, my mother was constantly telling me that I could do it, whatever it was I was trying to accomplish. She'd keep saying that I just needed to keep working on it, never give up, and eventually I'd reach my goal. As I got older, along with that encouragement came the words of wisdom about education. She kept instilling in me the great importance of getting a good education, and how necessary it would be for me to have a good job and be able to take care of myself. She knew I was different, very different, and she knew I didn't fit in. I knew it, too, although it wasn't something either one of us vocalized. It just was a normal way of life for us, pardon the pun!

Now that I'm an adult, my mother has admitted to me the many times she cried about things that happened to me, things that happened *because* I was different. I cried about them, too, but she insists she hurt more because I'm her child. In my support group, I hear the same thing from mothers that attend with their AS children.

What Educators Need to Know Regarding Students with Asperger's Syndrome, or Any Kind of Special Needs

I can vividly remember standing in the school gymnasium, with about forty other kids and the teachers, as teams for something like basketball were being selected. My palms would sweat, a lump would form in my throat, and tears would well in my eyes. I felt like a freak standing there, as the teams got bigger and the line of potential picks got smaller. I knew, without any doubt, that I'd be the last one standing there. And sure enough, there I'd be, standing all alone, everyone looking at me. Kids would point at me and laugh, yelling stuff like "loser" or "freak." Often times the teams would refuse to take me, and the teacher had to force me on one of them. As I slowly walked toward the group I was now to be a part of, I wished the ground would open up and just swallow me, taking me away from this too-frequent pain.

If I were an educator today, I would not allow students to do the selecting. Instead, I would create a different system. For example, put numbers in a hat and have each student pick a number, which would determine which team they were on. Additionally, I would *never* allow students to make fun of any student. I'd send them to the principal's office if they did. Looking back, I cannot believe what those teachers allowed to happen to me, or to any student who's different and the target of bullying.

> ## Power Point
>
> **Educators: For any kind of activity that involves teams, do not allow the students to choose their own teams. Instead, if there are to be two teams and there are, for example, twenty students, write A on ten pieces of paper and B on another ten. Place them in a container and have each student reach in and grab one paper, which will determine what team they are on. Also, emphasize to students that team work is all about helping one another and working together to accomplish the goal.**

Bullying Needs to End Once and For All

On the subject of bullying, it's still alive and well today; but actually, I see it as being a lot worse now than when I was a student. Today, kids use violence, and the victims are being pushed to the point of suicide. I blame many for this, though I start with the parents of the children who are doing the bullying. If a child is brought up to be a caring, polite individual, that child will never bully anyone. It's the kids of parents who think their child can do no wrong we need to worry about. Think of, for example, being in a restaurant, and the kid in the booth behind you keeps kicking the back of your seat. You turn around to kindly ask the parent to make the child stop, and the parent starts a fight with you, like you are the bad guy. These are the kids who will grow up to be bullies. They had good teachers.

It is of the utmost importance that you always maintain an open avenue of communication with your AS child. Even if they don't want to talk, do everything humanly possible to get them to open up daily about their day at school. You know everything that happens to them at home, but you don't know what happened to them at school. When something distressing happens at school, you need to know about it. It could develop into something dangerous, which you can prevent if you know about it. If a child is being bullied by someone or a group at school, the AS child might be scared to talk to his or her parent about it. Silence is the worst possible thing in this case.

My mother had a ritual when I came home from school each day. We'd sit at the kitchen table with a little snack, and she'd ask me about my day, about each class, and any interactions with peers or teachers that might have upset me. It was always a calm, quiet setting. No music, no TV, just our conversation. I'd look forward to it each day, as would any child, especially one with AS. No matter how busy your schedule is, arrange this type of session with your child. There should not be any distractions, and don't think that doing it while driving is a good substitute.

Shut off your cell phone too.

Power Point

If your child is the victim of bullying, immediately report it to the school and demand they do something about it. If they don't, do not hesitate to go to the police with it. Fortunately, laws are now being passed against bullying. Still, it is up to you, the parent, to seek out the avenue that will ultimately stop the bullying.

Ways to Build Self-Esteem

Throughout my whole life as an Aspie, it seemed that just about everyone was out to make me feel poorly about myself. When you are different, you are treated like a second-class citizen. People don't know anything about you, yet will decide to do something to degrade or humiliate you. Somehow, that makes them feel better. This applies to anyone who's different, whether it's Asperger's syndrome, the color of their skin, their body build, their religion, their culture, a problem with stuttering … Anything that makes them different from the people who set the standard of what is normal. It is the parents' job to constantly reinforce to their children their self-worth, that they are great, and to emphasize any special abilities or talents they possess. Encourage them to pursue a special interest if they have one; and if they don't, help them find one.

My passion for horses started at an early age, and is still present today. Looking back, I wonder what would have happened to me if I hadn't had my love of horses. I know I would have been extremely lonely. No one from school, and I'm talking elementary, junior high, and high school, ever wanted to be my friend. I did have the other kids at the stable, who were all around my own age, and all hooked on horses. We all hung out together at the barn. Of course, we talked about horses all the time, but we'd have fun brushing them, riding together, and simply sitting together after a ride. In the warm months, after we'd finished mucking out stalls, a group of us would walk about three miles to a Burger King, eat our burgers and fries, then walk back to the stable and ride for an hour. That was our idea of a good time. Another thing we did was walk over to a department store that was only about half a mile away and buy some white chocolate from the fancy candy shop inside the store. Outside by the main entrance, we'd get some hot dogs from the pushcart vendor, and then go sit on a bench and feast. If it was wintertime, the big parking lot would have huge snow piles from when they cleared the lot. I'm talking like fourteen-foot high snow piles. We'd climb up one and sit up there to eat our goodies. No one ever paid any attention to us up there. Maybe they never saw us.

Once I went on to college, the horse friends were no longer there. Out in the real world, I couldn't make friends, no matter what I did. I never could understand why—until I found out about Asperger's. I'm fifty-one as I write this, and it's only been in the last four months that I've had friends, and they also have Asperger's syndrome. I met them at the Asperger's support group that I started. My local newspaper published an article about me, and it also announced the date and location of my new group. My two new friends, a brother and sister, ages fifty-one and fifty, saw the article. The brother called me the day the story appeared, and we talked for nearly two hours. Fred and Marilou came to the first meeting, and we've become great friends since then.

When we get together, we've limited it to just ourselves. We want to be free to talk, to share our innermost feelings of living with AS. I feel like I've known Fred and Marilou my whole life. Other than my mother, I've never felt so at ease talking to anyone. I know they won't judge me or laugh at me, and they truly understand how I think. Having their friendship is incredible, yet it saddens me to realize that this is what normal people have their whole lives. In a way, I think I treasure my friendship with them both more than any normal person could ever even imagine. I also wonder if other people experience their friendships with such depth.

How to Start a Support Group

I would highly recommend to any parent of a child with AS, and to adults with AS, to research your area for an Asperger's support group. If there isn't one, start one!

I've read just about every book there is on AS, and I can tell you with all my heart that nothing, nothing at all, can take the place of being with others who have AS. They are the only ones who truly understand what it's like to walk in these Asperger's shoes. They will understand what it means for an Aspie to be totally overwhelmed by sensory overload at a grocery store. A normal person couldn't even begin to imagine the overwhelming sensation, an actual physical feeling of becoming ill, of feeling trapped, and of impending doom, just from being somewhere as mundane as a grocery store. This same feeling can occur in any public place where there are lots of people, lots of noise, and controlled chaos. We don't like to sit out in the open at restaurants, but instead will request a dimly lit corner booth. Personally, I cannot even go to any restaurant that plays loud music. If I walk into such an establishment, I make an about-face and go right back out the door.

> **Power Point**
>
> **Starting a support group is easier than you think. Contact your local newspaper and tell them you wish to start a support group for people with Asperger's syndrome, and you would like their help. Find an appropriate location to have the meetings, which should be held once a month. Select a particular day of the month and time, and a contact person with a phone number and e-mail address. I selected my group's day to be the second Saturday of each month, from 11 a.m. to 1 p.m. I am the contact person. I initially started having the meetings at a local library, but now have them at the hospital I work at.**

Avoiding Meltdowns with the Asperger Child

At our AS support group the other day, someone asked to recommend what a parent should do with a child that is getting overwhelmed while out in public, and is starting to have a meltdown. My immediate response was to get them to a quiet place. You have to get them away from the stimuli that are causing sensory overload. This is an absolute must. Whether you are a child or an adult with AS, when you start to feel like that, you simply must get somewhere quiet and calm, and preferably dimly lit. AS people do not like fluorescent lighting. Indirect lights are most calming. Following is an example of what not to do with an Asperger's child, in my opinion.

> **Power Point**
>
> **To help avoid meltdowns, ensure the child has the opportunity for quiet time to cool off his circuits. Remember, an AS brain is like a big search engine with lots of wires. When overloaded, it crashes!**

Don't Overschedule a Child with Asperger's Syndrome, or Yourself for That Matter

I highly advise parents to not overschedule children with Asperger's syndrome. By this I mean, don't plan more than one event in a day. Examples are birthday parties, the zoo, lessons such as soccer, swimming, golf, etc. The child needs down time to relax in a quiet place, away from all the stimulation. If there is too much stimulation, the child's circuits will overload, and this will manifest in angry outbursts. This is actually good advice for adults as well, not to overload yourself with too many things in a day. The danger from overload is particularly pronounced when the person, whether a child or adult, is tired. Everything becomes magnified, and the person will react differently to stimuli when tired, compared to how he reacts when he is rested.

Power Point

For parents, don't schedule your AS child for multiple events in one day, going from lesson to lesson, birthday parties, or sporting events, etc. In addition, they are being driven all day in a vehicle, and possibly eating fast food on the run. That is too much stress, and even if the child seems to be having fun, his stress will probably come out in temper tantrums or angry outbursts.

How to Make Friends

I'm going to talk about friends—or the lack of them. I've already discussed my newfound friends, but I've only found them a few months ago. Prior to that, for more than fifty years, I did not have any friends. As strange as it might sound, it really never bothered me. There are so many things I'd like to do and never enough time to do them, so I've never been bored. I've never sat around wishing I had a friend. I've heard other AS people say the same thing. Everyone is an individual, though, and some AS people might sit around wishing they had friends.

By all means, do things for your child to promote making friends, but don't be alarmed if it doesn't happen. They probably will also be more inclined to get involved in a sport that is an individual sport, like horseback riding, golfing, biking, and swimming, as opposed to anything that involves a team. If they do want to participate in a team sport, do encourage it. Always remember that you should not force a child to do a sport that he or she doesn't want to do, or is afraid of. That would be counterproductive, even dangerous.

From someone who's got AS, here's what I can tell you about trying to make friends. As I said earlier, I now have two friends, Marilou and her brother, Fred. I call us the three musketeers. We communicate extremely well, but our brains are all wired alike, and we know where the other is coming from. Now with normal people, their brains are not wired like mine. If I try to become friends with a neurotypical person, in a very short time I can recognize that they are feeling uncomfortable. I guess it's from a combination of my facial expressions, or lack of them, and the things I say and how I say them. I've studied neurotypical people my whole life, long before I knew I had AS. I did know I was different, and that I didn't, or couldn't, make all the facial expressions that neurotypical people make. I also don't know the art of manipulating people, but I can easily recognize it when other people are doing it. As a matter of fact, I can easily see through someone who is doing something bad or fraudulent. I have a sixth sense for that type of behavior, and have often thought I should have gone into investigative work for law enforcement.

What I find is that if I do try to make a friend, I quickly get bored, because I pretty much only want to talk about what I want to talk about! This is very common among AS people, including children. It has nothing to do with being selfish; it's just the way our brain functions. If it so happens that the person I'm talking to shares one of my interests, then by golly, I'll talk a lot with them. I'm also not into hanging out in bars, or any type of social gatherings, even at people's homes. This is very classic of someone with Asperger's syndrome. I will describe how I feel in those types of situations.

The last time I was at a big party was about eight years ago, a Christmas party thrown by the group I worked for at the time. I lasted a whopping forty-five minutes. It was held at a posh hotel on Pensacola Beach. I arrived around seven that morning, because I had reserved a room at the hotel with an early arrival time. I brought my mom along, so she could get to sit on the balcony and watch the Gulf of Mexico. We enjoyed ourselves for several hours after arriving, and then I took a nap and tried to relax. I felt anxious about going to the party, knowing it would be loud and there would be lots of people. I was coming up with a multitude of reasons not to attend, but I was going because all the employees were expected to go.

I arrived at the party at 8:30 p.m., as others were filtering in. As I entered the ballroom, the music was blasting so loudly, it hurt my ears. I was ready to leave right then. I continued walking in, looking around for a familiar face. There were already several hundred people there. The party was for the anesthesia department, the whole operating room staff, all the surgeons, and dozens of people I'd never seen before. I spotted one of the other anesthetists and her husband. I made my way over to them, joining them in the food line for the buffet tables. We were way back in the line, which seemed to not move. Idle conversation was the entertainment during the lengthy wait. The whole time I kept thinking that I'd rather be up in my room watching the waves roll in, in peace and quiet. By the time we arrived at the food tables, there wasn't much left. A server told us to hold tight; refills were coming momentarily. She was right. About two minutes later, tons of food was brought out, nice things like crab claws, jumbo shrimp, and other delicious food. I put a few items on my plate, and we all made our way over to an empty table to sit down and eat. The music from the DJ was so loud, we all practically had to scream to talk to each other. I didn't say too much, but my throat was hoarse in no time flat.

I looked over by the stage where the DJ was, and saw a mirror ball hanging over it. The flashing lights it produced immediately made me feel like I was going to pass out. It was time to depart the party and get back upstairs to my room. I quickly said good-bye to my coworker and made my way through the crowd to the door. On the way through the ballroom, I noticed a partygoer leaning over and throwing up all over the nice rug, which I later learned was from drinking too much. Her boyfriend was holding her long brown hair back from her face. I thought, *This is what society considers normal.* I was glad I wasn't normal. Once up in the quiet of my hotel room, I lay on the bed for about twenty minutes to calm my brain down. Then I was able to sit out on the balcony with my mom and listen to the peaceful drone of the waves rolling in. I recounted to her my party disaster. To this day I wonder what normal people get out of those situations.

My advice is to try and meet other's with Asperger's syndrome, as you immediately have something very significant in common with them and will feel comfortable to interact with them.

Get out There and Do Volunteer Work

I've always done volunteer work of one kind or another. It makes me feel good to do things to help others less fortunate than me. Whether I'm taking up collections for a local homeless shelter, food bank, or animal shelter, I feel good about helping out. Years ago, I was a hospital volunteer. When I lived in New York City, I helped at a soup kitchen. I learned a lot about life and people doing this kind of work.

Think of some group that you would like to help and see if they need volunteers. There are things like Habitat for Humanity, local hospitals, homeless shelters, the Red Cross, hospices. The list is endless. Just get out there and do something, even if it's only a few hours a month. It will do two things. First, you will be helping others; and second, you'll also be helping yourself.

Learning to Drive with Asperger's Syndrome

When an AS child learns to drive, it isn't the same as it is for neurotypical kids. Driving a car entails a lot of things happening all at once. Steering, deciding if you need the gas pedal or brake, watching for traffic, watching for traffic lights … You get the picture. To someone with AS, this is totally overwhelming. Remember, some AS people are not good at multitasking. Driving is multitasking at its worst, because your life is at stake, as well as those of others on the road.

More than likely, the child will receive driving lessons at school during high school. Neurotypical kids will be so excited that they will now be able to drive, but the AS kid will be very nervous about it, and might announce that he doesn't want to start driving yet. They feel overwhelmed and their circuits become overloaded. What you can do is, early on a Sunday morning, take the child to the parking lot of a mall, when it's totally empty, and have them sit in the driver's seat for a while, just to get them comfortable sitting behind the wheel. You will need to dissect each component of driving, starting from holding the steering wheel to checking mirrors, all while being parked. Take it slow. Maybe just go over a few points that day and plan another lesson the following week. Be sure to observe that the child isn't getting overwhelmed. Ask him to repeat the steps as you go. All this must be done while parked, no matter how many times you have to go to the parking lot. The child must be familiar with the mechanics of driving while at a standstill, before you can expect him to be comfortable driving out on the road, where other cars are moving all around them and traffic lights are changing color, and people are doing stupid, careless things on the road.

When I learned to drive in high school, I was terrified I was going to get killed. I realized I was overwhelmed by the whole process, and just didn't want to do it. Fortunately, my mother drove me everywhere I needed to go. This, of course, set me up for ridicule by other students and, once I was in the workplace, by coworkers.

I started driving full-time ten years ago. To this day, however, I still don't like it, and I feel overwhelmed most of the time. I'm especially not happy driving at night when it's raining, and going down roads that have a lot of traffic lights and businesses along them. All the lights reflecting on the wet roads start my circuits burning up in my head. It looks like a French Impressionist painting, but I'd rather be admiring it hanging on a wall, rather than driving in it. I also drive "by the book." I don't speed, tailgate, jump red lights or stop signs, all of which too many other drivers are doing. That adds to my anxiety.

Power Point

When your child is going to learn to drive, let him take the learning process at his own speed. Do not try to rush him. Sooner or later he will do it, but it's got to be at the pace he feels comfortable at. It might be years before he is ready, or he may never be ready. Don't worry about what other kids are doing. Focus on the fact that you want your child to be safe.

Difficulty Learning to Ride a Bike

Because of coordination issues, children with Asperger's syndrome will usually have difficulty learning to ride a bike. Do not panic. AS children will learn to ride bikes when they are ready to. Don't try to force them, and don't compare them to other children. Sooner or later they will learn, on their own terms.

The Need for Proper Diet, Exercise, and Sleep

Eating healthy and getting regular physical activity and enough sleep is important to everyone, but more so to people with Asperger's syndrome, in my opinion. Because stress is very common, our bodies needs to be at optimal functioning to be best able to deal with it. Eating a healthy diet, getting some form of regular exercise, and the proper amount of sleep is extremely important to your overall feeling of well-being. Nothing can take the place of physically feeling great. That enables you to handle the mental aspects of AS much better. Relaxation also fits in, as that also plays an important role in your well-being. Be sure to do something each and every day to relax, even if it's only for fifteen minutes. I like to turn on my Himalayan salt rock lamp, which is a bowl made of Himalayan salt rocks and filled with the same rocks, with a small light inside it. When lit, it exudes a peaceful, soft orange glow. I'll put on my Yanni *Love Songs* CD, or my American Indian flute and drum CD, and play it quietly as I look at the lamp. I concentrate on my breathing to make it slow and relaxed. In a short time, I feel rested and refreshed. I make sure during that time that I do not allow any thoughts in my mind. That time is strictly to cleanse my body and soul.

Chapter 16:

Recipe for Making Lemonade

In closing, I want to have a heart-to-heart talk with my fellow Aspies. Yes, we're all different from the rest of the world, but learn to embrace that fact. Don't focus on the negative aspects of Asperger's—and yes, I know there are negative aspects—but instead focus on the positive things. You were born this way, and nothing is going to change that. You can work on areas to improve yourself, and you will, because you want to. Your brain has the capacity to focus on things in a laserlike fashion, so use that ability to its fullest.

There are many famous people who revolutionized the world who had Asperger's. If those people had not been different and hadn't accomplished what they did, where would our world be today? It was their dreams and unrelenting drive that took them to the top.

Believe in yourself. Know that you can do something that you put your mind to. Work hard at what you choose, and eventually you will accomplish your dream. Be creative. If one way of trying something doesn't succeed, dream up another path to get there. Just keep on going and never give up.

I recently was invited to a university to be a guest speaker to a group of students with Asperger's syndrome. The professor who was sponsoring the lecture was of Asian descent. I was talking to her before my lecture, and mentioned my thoughts on employment—that when you have AS, you need to be the best at what you do, to compensate for the negative social aspects. She said she knew what I meant, because she struggles with a different type of issue, but the same problem. She said that being an Asian woman, she has to work harder at her job than a white man or woman applying for the same job. Her résumé needs to be bigger and better than her competition. Unfortunately, that's true. This is how society is. Nothing is ever going to change that. You just need to learn coping strategies to navigate life.

I mentioned that little interaction, because I want to emphasize to all Aspies that there are other things out there in life that people have to deal with, and having AS isn't the worst thing that can happen to you. Having been in the medical profession for twenty-three years, I have seen a wide variety of people who have either suffered a tragedy, or were born with a terrible handicap. Most of them make the best of it. You can too.

Don't be too hard on yourself. You think differently. It's okay. There are millions of people out there with Asperger's syndrome, and we all need to unite. One thing that does bothers me is that I see too many people with AS who just sit around and dwell on it, focusing on the fact that they are different, and simply stalling out on life. Historically, there have been some ethnic groups that have fought adversity to advance to where they stand in society today. Those peoples, however, had a lot worse adversity. They went through terrible torture and abuse, but they kept on going. They fought for their rights. And they won. It took a lot of struggle on their part to get there, but they never quit the climb.

My dream is twofold. I want to educate the world about what Asperger's syndrome is, and I want everyone with AS to feel like they belong here on this planet. When people start to understand that we are born with AS and that is how our brains work, they will be more accepting of us. Knowledge is power. Society's knowledge of AS will empower us.

I admit that when I was younger, I often felt like I was from another planet, like I was a space alien. Then, as I got older and wiser, I came to embrace the fact that I'm different. I would never have done all the exciting things I've done had I been "normal." Now that I have traveled this long journey, I want to share my knowledge with others with AS, to help them realize that it's really okay to be different. In fact, it's great. I feel like I belong to an elite group of people. Aside from all the famous people with AS, there are plenty of others out there who might not be famous, but are gifted and talented in many ways. It is this special group of people who have changed the world, who have revolutionized it; the people who dreamed big and worked hard until their dreams became reality. I am proud to be one of them.

So get started today making your own lemonade. Think positively. Yes, you *can* do it. Be proud that you are different. Unleash the power of your mind to accomplish whatever you set out to do, no matter how small or big your dream is. The key ingredient for my recipe is simple: it is perseverance, the drive to keep on going and never give up. You will achieve your dream, whatever that may be.

One of the highlights of my military aviation experience was getting to talk with the Commanding Officer/Flight Leader of the U.S. Navy Blue Angels, Cdr. Patrick Driscoll. He was extremely gracious and answered my many questions, and gave me great insight into what being the # 1 Blue Angel Flight Leader is all about.

VERY SPECIAL THANKS

Brett W. Turner, PsyD, Clinical Neuropsychologist - My most sincerest thanks to Dr. Turner for his unwavering support and exceptional advice. His expertise in Asperger's syndrome was a benefit when I first visited him to get formally diagnosed with Asperger's syndrome. He then provided much needed work-related advice and guidance.

Lee Day, PhD - Many thanks for her help at my workplace to teach my employer what Asperger syndrome is, and enlighten them about how Asperger's think and act.

Joe Weber - New York Times Bestselling author, and former Marine Fighter pilot. Visit Joe at www.joewebernovels.com

"If a man does not keep pace with his companions, perhaps it is because he hears a different drummer. Let him step to the music he hears, however measured or far away."

Henry David Thoreau, Walden. 1854.

CPSIA information can be obtained at www.ICGtesting.com
Printed in the USA
LVOW131751280212

270834LV00006B/199/P